200 low

200 low fat dishes

hamlyn **all color**

Maria Ricci

An Hachette Livre UK company
www.hachettelivre.co.uk

First published in Great Britain in 2008 by Hamlyn,
a division of Octopus Publishing Group Ltd
2–4 Heron Quays, London E14 4JP
www.octopusbooksusa.com

Copyright © Octopus Publishing Group Ltd 2008

Distributed in the U.S. and Canada by Octopus Books USA:
c/o Hachette Book Group USA
237 Park Avenue
New York NY 10017

Some of the recipes in this book have previously appeared
in other books published by Hamlyn.

All rights reserved. No part of this work may be reproduced
or utilized in any form or by any means, electronic or
mechanical, including photocopying, recording or by any
information storage and retrieval system, without the prior
written permission of the publisher.

ISBN: 978-0-600-61873-7

A CIP catalog record for this book is available from the
Library of Congress

Printed and bound in China

1 2 3 4 5 6 7 8 9 10

All recipes contain 12 g of fat per serving or less (not including
serving suggestions)

Standard level spoon measurements are used in all recipes.

Ovens should be preheated to the specified temperature—if
using a fan-assisted oven, follow the manufacturer's
instructions for adjusting the time and the temperature.

Fresh herbs should be used unless otherwise stated.

Medium eggs should be used unless otherwise stated.

The Food and Drug Administration advises that eggs should
not be eaten raw. This book contains some dishes made with
raw or lightly cooked eggs. It is prudent for vulnerable people
such as pregnant and nursing mothers, invalids, the elderly,
babies, and young children to avoid uncooked or lightly
cooked dishes made with eggs. Once prepared, these dishes
should be kept refrigerated and used promptly.

This book includes dishes made with nuts and nut derivatives.
It is advisable for those with known allergic reactions to nuts
and nut derivatives and those who may be potentially
vulnerable to these allergies, such as pregnant and nursing
mothers, invalids, the elderly, babies, and children, to avoid
dishes made with nuts and nut oils and to check the labels of
pre-prepared ingredients.

contents

introduction

introduction

We all know that we need to take care with what we eat. In the long term, sticking to a healthy diet requires us to look beyond the celebrity diets and weight-loss programs. These may help lose a few pounds in the short term, but will not give a foundation for lasting healthy habits.

Changing habits

The most important change we can make is to reduce the amount of fat we consume. Eliminating all fat is unrealistic and in fact unhealthy, because fat is essential in the supply of vitamins A, D, E, and K and for the production of new cells and hormones. However, permanently lowering the amount of fat in our diet should be the aim of all of us.

There is no shortage of advice about what constitutes a low-fat diet, and books

and magazines are full of articles about good fats versus bad fats, foods to avoid, cooking methods to use, and even what size plate to put it all on. For most of us, putting this advice into practice is difficult. Translating the wealth of information into day-to-day cooking and changing the habits of a lifetime needs something more than a couple of paragraphs of nutritional science.

Going low fat

How can you reduce the amount of fat in your diet? What does it mean to make healthy choices? The recipes in this book will help to translate all the confusing advice into real food and well-balanced meals.

Following a reduced-fat diet does require a change in attitudes at the outset. Eating healthily means looking in a new way at how you shop and eat. Your aim is regular, well-balanced meals that contain enough starchy foods, vegetables, and protein—a third of each on the plate is a good guide. Nutritious meals will take away the desire for unhealthy, fat-rich snacks in between.

Cooking for a family can be difficult, as you have to satisfy a range of different needs and tastes. Try sitting down with your family and selecting a few recipes from this book to sample. Remember that most recipes can be simplified for small children and toddlers.

Shopping for low-fat cooking

Making a list before you shop will help you to walk past the high-fat ready meals and ignore snacks and candy. Many ingredients are available in healthier versions. Full-fat dairy products, for example, are easily substituted with the low-fat versions: choose skim or lowfat milk instead of whole milk and nonfat or low-fat yogurt instead of whole milk products. If you select thick light cream you won't miss heavy cream. Sunflower spread can be used instead of butter in most types of baking.

Look again at the amazing array of fruit and vegetables available. Experiment with new salad leaves and have fun with fruit. Pineapples and mangoes contain just as much vitamin C as oranges and kiwifruit. Although buying locally produced, in-season fruit and vegetables is the ideal, the freezer section of your supermarket will also offer more unusual items to tempt the family. Soybeans, baby fava beans, and corn freeze well, and frozen fruits, such as raspberries and blueberries, are wonderful in winter desserts.

The meat counter offers some healthy alternatives. Pork can be one of the leanest cuts available if you choose tenderloin and not pork belly. Lean ground pork is also widely available, or you could buy tenderloin and process it yourself. If you prefer lamb,

look out for leg steaks rather than the fattier chops.

Chicken breast is the leanest part of the bird, and you can reduce the fat content still further by buying skinless cuts or removing the skin yourself. Turkey is also a low-fat option, so consider replacing the ham in your lunchbox sandwiches with cold cooked turkey.

Don't forget to buy healthy cooking oil. An oil spray will transform pan-fried meals into low-fat versions. If you cannot find a spray, wipe away excess oil from your skillet with paper towels before frying onions or garlic.

Another easy way to reduce your intake of saturated fat is to eat fish instead of meat two or three times a week. Supermarkets often have excellent fish counters, and frozen

fish is widely available. A simple fresh fish fillet, seasoned and quickly broiled, is the basis of a delicious and healthy meal.

Ready-made cakes and cookies contain a lot of fat—often the "wrong" kind. Walk straight past the cookies and on to the home baking section. Although your home-baked cakes and cookies will contain some fat, you can control the type and choose sunflower and low-fat spreads.

Equipment

A steamer is a good investment if you are aiming to reduce your fat intake. Steamers quickly and cleanly cook several things at a time and all over a single heat source. You will find that steamed vegetables have such a great flavor that you will not miss the salt, and none of the goodness is lost in the water.

A large, good-quality, nonstick skillet or wok with a lid is invaluable. A nonstick pan

enables you to dry-fry foods without fear of them sticking, although bear in mind that the temperature for dry-frying has to be just right: too low, and the food sticks to the pan; too high, and it will burn without cooking. You will need nonstick utensils to protect the surface of the pan.

A chargrill pan allows you to transform a simple fish fillet into a Mediterranean delight. It will also cook chops and other cuts of meat while letting the fat drain away. Make sure the pan is really hot: allow about 10 minutes to preheat the pan. Buy a heavy pan that will hold the heat well. Operating on the same principle—but easier to clean—are the low-fat grilling machines. All types enable cooking while draining excess fat away.

Methods

If you regularly fry foods ask yourself if they can be broiled or roasted instead. Set your lamb chop or steak on a broiler rack and the fat will drain off into the roasting pan below. Broiling or roasting also makes it easier to add flavors. For example, you can top a piece of salmon with lemon slices or add some chopped herbs to the basting juices of chicken fillets.

Deep-fried vegetables can often be baked. For healthier French fries, toss fries or wedges in a little oil and seasoning and bake in a preheated oven, 400°F, for about 20 minutes.

Plan ahead and make casseroles and stews the day before. If you leave them overnight in the refrigerator, the flavor will improve and the fat will solidify at the surface so that you can easily skim it off.

Serving suggestions

When you serve your delicious, well-balanced, low-fat meal, you can make it even more appealing with a few tweaks at the table. Changing the size of serving plates is often cited as a good place to start if you want to reduce your overall intake of calories. A medium-size portion on a small plate will look more filling than the same portion on a large plate.

If you like to add butter to baked potatoes, try offering whole-milk yogurt instead. Instead of serving bread with butter, simply offer it without butter or with oil to dip into. If you spread jelly on hot toast you will not miss the butter. A tasty raspberry coulis, widely available from supermarkets, will be better for you and your family than a spoonful of heavy cream on a fresh fruit salad.

Rather than offering ready-made mayonnaise try a range of relishes or chutneys. Mango chutney goes happily with many recipes and lime pickle is an excellent accompaniment for salmon. Use tomato relish to pep up your burgers.

The key to low-fat cooking and eating is to include lots of flavor to replace the richness of the fat. Serve interesting vegetables and the absence of a creamy sauce will be unremarked. Try unusual combinations, such as zucchini and red sweet pepper, runner beans and green beans, to tempt jaded taste buds. Toss baked sweet peppers through steamed potatoes, or try finishing off steamed vegetables with chopped chives and parsley and a little grated lemon.

Once you have started to change your habits, you will not regret the decision to cook and eat a lower fat diet. When you take in unnecessary extra fat, your body has to expend energy to process and store it. As soon as you reduce your fat intake, you will immediately feel the difference in your energy levels. And more energy means that you can be more active, thereby further improving your overall health.

Enjoy the recipes in this book, and may your low-fat regime last.

everyday

spicy pork, fried rice, & greens

Serves **4**
Preparation time **15 minutes**,
  plus marinating
Cooking time **20 minutes**

1 cup **easy-cook
  basmati rice**
3 tablespoons **hoisin sauce**
2 **garlic cloves**, crushed
2 inch piece **fresh ginger
  root**, grated
1 **red chili**, sliced
1 **star anise**
1 tablespoon **sun-dried
  tomato paste**
10 oz **pork tenderloin**, cut
  into thin strips
sunflower oil spray
1 **red onion**, chopped
4 oz **cabbage** or **collard
  greens**, finely chopped
1 **carrot**, finely sliced
toasted sesame seeds,
  to serve

Cook the rice in boiling salted water for 16–18 minutes. Drain and set aside.

Meanwhile, mix together the hoisin sauce, garlic, ginger, chili, star anise, and tomato paste. Toss the pork in the mixture, cover, and set aside for up to 1 hour.

Heat a wok over high heat and spray with oil. Remove the pork from the marinade (discard the remainder) and cook the meat in the wok for about 1 minute. Stir in the onion, cabbage, and carrot, then the rice. Toss and stir everything together over high heat for about 3 minutes, until the rice is hot. Sprinkle with sesame seeds and serve.

For hoisin lamb with stir-fry noodles, use 10 oz lamb fillet instead of pork and omit the rice and tomato paste. Marinate and stir-fry the lamb with the vegetables as above. Then add 3 x 5 oz packages straight-to-wok rice noodles (or dried rice noodles, cooked according to the package instructions) and stir-fry for about 1 minute, until hot. Sprinkle with chopped fresh cilantro leaves instead of sesame seeds and serve.

chicken satay

Serves **4**
Preparation time **10 minutes**,
  plus marinating
Cooking time **10 minutes**

1½ tablespoons **smooth**
  peanut butter
½ cup **soy sauce**
½ cup **lime juice**
2½ tablespoons **curry powder**
2 **garlic cloves**, chopped
1 teaspoon **hot pepper sauce**
6 boneless, skinless **chicken**
  breasts, about 4 oz each,
  cubed

Presoak 12 wooden skewers in warm water. Mix together the peanut butter, soy sauce, lime juice, curry powder, garlic, and hot pepper sauce in a large bowl.

Put the chicken in the marinade and allow to marinate in the refrigerator for about 8 hours or overnight.

Thread the chicken onto skewers and transfer to a foil-lined broiler pan. Cook under a preheated hot broiler for 5 minutes on each side.

For pork satay, marinate cubed pork in a mixture of 3 crushed garlic cloves, ½ teaspoon each ground cumin and ground cinnamon, 1 teaspoon each ground coriander and turmeric, 2 teaspoons superfine sugar, 2 tablespoons lime juice, 4 finely sliced scallions, and 2 tablespoons olive oil. Thread onto skewers and cook as above.

chicken with lemon & parsley

Serves **4**

Preparation time **5 minutes**

Cooking time **8 minutes**

4 boneless, skinless **chicken
    breasts**, about 4 oz each
1 tablespoon **olive oil**
2 tablespoons **butter**
2 tablespoons **lemon juice**
3 tablespoons chopped
    parsley
1 tablespoon chopped
    oregano
salt and pepper
lemon wedges, to serve

Use a sharp knife to cut each chicken breast in half horizontally. Transfer the chicken to a foil-lined broiler pan and season.

Put the oil, butter, lemon juice, parsley, and oregano in a small pan and heat until the butter is melted. Spoon or brush this mix over the chicken.

Broil the chicken in batches under a preheated hot broiler for about 4 minutes until just cooked and still succulent. Serve immediately with lemon wedges and, if desired, whole-wheat pasta.

For spicy chicken salad wraps, add a seeded chopped red chili to the mixture with the parsley and oregano and broil as above. Warm 8 wheat tortillas in the bottom of the broiler compartment while cooking the chicken. Mix 3 cups each watercress and arugula and divide among the tortillas. Slice the chicken thinly and arrange on the leaves, then roll up and serve with lemon wedges.

beef & pepper kebabs

Serves **4**

Preparation time **15 minutes**, plus marinating

Cooking time **15 minutes**

13 oz **steak**, sirloin or top round

1 **red bell pepper**, cored and seeded

1 **green bell pepper**, cored and seeded

1 teaspoon crushed **coriander seeds**

3 tablespoons **vegetable oil**

¼ cup chopped **cilantro**

1 **red chili**, seeded and chopped

1 **garlic clove**, crushed

2 tablespoons **lime juice**

4 **chapattis**

salt and pepper

Presoak 8 wooden skewers in warm water. Cut the beef and peppers into 1 inch cubes.

Mix together the coriander seeds, 2 tablespoons oil, and half the chopped cilantro in a bowl and season to taste. Add the beef and peppers and toss to coat.

Thread the beef and peppers onto the skewers, cover, and refrigerate for up to 1 hour.

Mix together the remaining cilantro and oil with the chili, garlic, and lime juice to make a dressing, season to taste and set aside.

Broil the skewers under a preheated hot broiler for 15 minutes, turning often and basting with the juices. Warm the chapattis under the broiler.

Serve 2 skewers per person on a hot chapatti and drizzle over the cilantro dressing.

For lime & chive couscous, to serve as an accompaniment, put 1⅓ cups couscous in a bowl and pour on enough boiling water to cover it by 1 inch. Cover the bowl and allow to stand for about 5 minutes, until the water is absorbed and the couscous is plump. Stir in the grated zest and juice of 1 lime and 3 tablespoons snipped fresh chives. Serve topped with the kebabs and the cilantro dressing.

haddock parcels & coconut rice

Serves **4**
Preparation time **15 minutes**
Cooking time **20 minutes**

4 **haddock fillets**, about
  5 oz each
4 tablespoons chopped
  cilantro
1 **red chili**, chopped
1 **shallot**, finely sliced
1 **lime**, sliced, plus extra lime
  halves to serve
2 **lemon grass stalks**,
  1 roughly chopped and
  1 bashed
1 cup **Thai jasmine rice**
2 fresh or dried **kaffir lime
  leaves**
3 tablespoons **reduced-fat
  coconut milk**

Cut 4 pieces of nonstick parchment paper, each
12 inches square. Put a haddock fillet in the center
of each piece and arrange some of the cilantro, chili,
shallot, lime, and chopped lemon grass stalk evenly
over each. Wrap them up into neat parcels.

Transfer the parcels to a baking sheet and cook in
a preheated oven, 350°F, for 20 minutes.

Meanwhile, put the rice in a pan with 1¾ cups water,
the bashed lemon grass stalk, and the lime leaves.
Cover and simmer for 12 minutes. When the rice is
cooked and the water absorbed, stir in the coconut
milk. Serve with the haddock parcels, with some extra
lime halves.

For salmon parcels with sesame rice, use 5 oz
portions of skinless salmon fillet instead of the
haddock. Use lemon slices instead of lime and omit
the lemon grass. Sprinkle a few drops of sesame oil
over each salmon portion and cook as above. Omit
the lime leaves and coconut milk from the rice. Fork
2 tablespoons toasted sesame seeds and 2 chopped
scallions into the cooked rice and serve with the
salmon, adding lemon wedges for additional zest.

blackened salmon with salsa

Serves **4**
Preparation time **15 minutes**
Cooking time **8 minutes**

3 tablespoons **Cajun
 seasoning**
1 teaspoon **dried oregano**
4 **salmon fillets**, about 3 oz
 each
sunflower oil, to brush
lime wedges, to garnish

Cajun salsa
13½ oz can **black-eyed peas**,
 rinsed and drained
2 tablespoons **olive oil**
1 **avocado**, peeled, pitted,
 and chopped
2 **plum tomatoes**, finely
 chopped
1 **yellow bell pepper**, seeded
 and finely chopped
2 tablespoons **lime juice**
salt and pepper

Mix together the Cajun seasoning and oregano in a
shallow bowl.

Brush the salmon on both sides with a little oil and
coat with the spice mix, making sure the fish is
completely covered. Set aside.

Meanwhile, make the salsa by mixing together all the
ingredients in a bowl. Season to taste and set aside.

Cook the salmon in a preheated, dry skillet for
4 minutes on each side.

Slice the salmon and serve with the salsa, with lime
wedges to garnish.

For salsa verde, drain and finely chop 6 anchovy
fillets in oil and combine them with 3 tablespoons
chopped basil, 3 tablespoons chopped parsley or
chives, 2 teaspoons roughly chopped capers,
2 teaspoons Dijon mustard, 3 tablespoons olive
oil, and 1½ tablespoons white wine vinegar.

shrimp skewers with relish

Serves **4**
Preparation time **10 minutes**
Cooking time **10 minutes**

4 **gherkins**, finely chopped
⅓ cup finely chopped
   cucumber
1 **shallot**, finely chopped
3 tablespoons **olive oil**
1½ tablespoons **white wine**
   vinegar
1 tablespoon roughly
   chopped **dill**
13 oz raw **jumbo shrimp**
salt and pepper

Presoak 12 wooden skewers in warm water. Mix together the gherkins, cucumber, and shallot in a small dish. In a separate bowl mix together the oil, vinegar, and dill and season to taste.

Thread about 4 shrimp onto each skewer and cook under a preheated hot broiler for about 10 minutes, turning once or twice, until the shrimp are thoroughly cooked through.

Arrange the shrimp skewers on 4 plates. Pour the dressing over the gherkin mixture and stir to mix. Spoon the relish over the shrimp and serve with new potatoes, if desired.

For scallop skewers with cucumber & avocado relish, use 16 small scallops without roes instead of the shrimp. Halve, pit, peel, and dice 2 firm but ripe avocados and mix them with the cucumber, omitting the gherkins. Dress the relish as soon as the avocado is diced. Brush the scallops very lightly with a little olive oil and broil for 2–3 minutes on each side, until just firm and opaque. Serve the scallops and relish with new potatoes or rice.

flounder with herby coconut crust

Serves **4**
Preparation time **10 minutes**
Cooking time **15 minutes**

⅓ cup **shredded coconut**

1 cup **bread crumbs**

2 tablespoons chopped
   chives

pinch of **paprika**

4 **skinless flounder fillets**

salt and pepper

lime wedges, to serve

Mix together the coconut, bread crumbs, chives, and paprika and season to taste.

Arrange the fish fillets on a baking sheet, top each one with some of the coconut mixture and cook in a preheated oven, 350°F, for 15 minutes.

Serve the fish with lime wedges and accompanied with baked potatoes and an arugula salad, if desired.

For lemon sole with an almond crust, substitute the flounder fillets with 4 skinless lemon sole fillets. In the topping, use ½ cup slivered almonds instead of coconut. Serve the fish with new potatoes, watercress, and lemon wedges.

penne with roasted tomatoes

Serves **4**
Preparation time **15 minutes**
Cooking time **15 minutes**

1 lb **cherry tomatoes**, halved
2 tablespoons **olive oil**
2 **garlic cloves**, finely
   chopped
4–5 stems of **rosemary**
large pinch of **paprika** or
   chili powder
12 oz dried **whole-wheat**
   penne
2 tablespoons **balsamic**
   vinegar
4 tablespoons **low-fat crème**
   fraîche or **ricotta**
salt and pepper
Parmesan cheese shavings,
   to serve

Put the tomatoes in a roasting pan, drizzle over the oil and sprinkle with the garlic, the torn leaves from 3 rosemary stems, paprika or chili powder, and a little seasoning. Cook in a preheated oven, 400°F, for 15 minutes or until just softened.

Meanwhile, cook the pasta in a large saucepan of boiling water for 10–12 minutes or until just tender, then drain.

Spoon the balsamic vinegar into the tomatoes, add the drained pasta and crème fraîche or ricotta and toss together. Spoon the penne into bowls and top with Parmesan shavings.

For penne with tomatoes, pine nuts, & raisins, omit the paprika or chili powder and add a handful each of pine nuts and raisins to the roasting pan, then proceed as above. Serve sprinkled with diced mozzarella rather than Parmesan and allow the cheese to soften before serving.

lamb & prune tagine with barley

Serves **4**
Preparation time **15 minutes**
Cooking time **1–1¼ hours**

olive oil spray
1¼ lb lean diced **lamb**
1 **red onion**, chopped
1 **carrot**, peeled and chopped
1 teaspoon **paprika**
1 teaspoon **ground coriander**
1 teaspoon **fennel seeds**
1¼ inch **cinnamon stick**
2 **garlic cloves**, crushed
2 **bay leaves**
3 cups **chicken stock**
½ cup **dried prunes**
13 oz can **chopped tomatoes**
⅓ cup **pearl barley**
½ cup chopped **cilantro,** plus
   extra sprigs to garnish
2 tablespoons **lime juice**
2⅓ cups **couscous**
salt and pepper

Heat a large saucepan or 8 cup flameproof casserole, spray lightly with oil and cook the lamb briefly, in batches if necessary, until brown. Remove the lamb with a slotted spoon, add the onion and carrot to the pan and cook briefly to brown. Return the lamb, stir in all the remaining ingredients, except for the cilantro, lime juice, and couscous, and season to taste.

Simmer covered for 1 hour or until the lamb is tender. At the end of the cooking time, stir in the cilantro and lime juice.

Meanwhile, cook the couscous according to the instructions on the package and set aside for 5 minutes. Serve the hot tagine over the couscous and garnish with cilantro sprigs.

For pork & apricot tagine, replace the lamb with the same quantity of diced pork and substitute the dried prunes with dried apricots. Toast a generous handful of split almonds in a dry pan over a medium heat, then stir into the casserole along with the other ingredients.

turkey burgers & sweet potatoes

Serves **4**

Preparation time **15 minutes**,
  plus chilling

Cooking time **40 minutes**

1½ lb **sweet potatoes**,
  washed but unpeeled and
  cut into wedges

2 tablespoons **sunflower oil**

1 lb **ground turkey**

½ **red bell pepper**, cored,
  seeded, and chopped

11 oz can **corn**, rinsed and
  drained

1 **onion**, chopped

1 **egg**, beaten

6 **whole-wheat bread rolls**

salad leaves and **tomato**
  slices

salt and pepper

Toss the potato wedges in 1 tablespoon oil, season to taste, and bake in a preheated oven, 400°F, for 30 minutes, turning after 15 minutes.

Meanwhile, in a large bowl mix together the turkey with the bell pepper, corn, and onion. Season to taste and add the egg. Shape the mixture into 6 burgers and refrigerate until ready to cook.

Heat the remaining oil in a shallow skillet over medium heat. Add the burgers, 3 at a time, and cook for 2 minutes on each side until brown. Transfer to a baking sheet and finish cooking in the oven, below the potato wedges, for 15 minutes or until cooked through.

Cut the rolls in half and cook them, cut side down, in the hot pan. Put a few salad leaves and tomato slices in each roll, add a burger, and serve them with the sweet potato wedges.

For lamb & chickpea burgers, replace the turkey with 10 oz ground lamb. Take 2 x 13 oz cans chickpeas and mash them roughly with a fork. When mixing all the ingredients, omit the corn and replace it with the mashed chickpeas.

chicken with red kidney beans

Serves **4**
Preparation time **15 minutes**
Cooking time **20–25 minutes**

sunflower oil spray
1 **onion**, roughly chopped
1 **red bell pepper**, cored,
 seeded, and roughly
 chopped
1 **garlic clove**, halved
8 oz boneless, skinless
 chicken thighs, cut into
 1¼ inch dice
2 teaspoons **mild chili
 powder**
1 cup **easy-cook long-grain
 rice**
13½ oz can **red kidney beans**,
 rinsed and drained
12½ oz can **cherry tomatoes
 in natural juice**
¾ cup **chicken stock**
salt and pepper

To serve
cilantro leaves, roughly
 chopped
lime wedges

Heat a large skillet with a flameproof handle and lightly spray with oil. Add the onion, bell pepper, garlic, and chicken and cook, stirring, over a medium heat for 3 minutes.

Add the chili powder, rice, beans, tomatoes, and stock to the pan, season to taste, bring to a boil and simmer for 15 minutes.

When the rice and chicken are cooked, spoon as much of the chicken on top of the rice as you can and cook under a preheated hot broiler until golden.

Serve with chopped cilantro and lime wedges.

For chicken & chickpea casserole, replace the kidney beans with a 13½ oz can chickpeas and add ½ teaspoon ground cinnamon, the juice of ½ lemon, and the other ingredients at the second stage. Cook as above, then garnish with mint leaves rather than cilantro and lime wedges.

chili pork with pineapple rice

Serves **4**

Preparation time **20 minutes**,
  plus marinating

Cooking time **15 minutes**

2 tablespoons **sunflower oil**

2 tablespoons **lime juice**

2 **garlic cloves**, crushed

1 **red chili**, seeded and finely
  chopped

10 oz **pork tenderloin**, cubed

1 cup **Thai fragrant rice**

6 **scallions**, finely sliced

½ cup peeled and diced
  pineapple

½ **red onion**, cut into wedges

1 **lime**, cut into wedges

salt and pepper

ready-made **sweet chili
  sauce**, to serve

Presoak 8 wooden skewers in warm water. Mix together the oil, lime juice, garlic, chili, and salt and pepper in a bowl, add the pork and stir to coat. Cover and refrigerate for at least 1 hour.

Meanwhile, cook the rice in lightly salted boiling water for 12–15 minutes or according to the instructions on the package. Drain and stir through the scallions and pineapple.

Thread the pork onto the skewers, alternating it with onion and lime wedges, and cook under a preheated hot broiler for about 10 minutes, turning frequently and basting with the remaining marinade, until the pork is cooked through.

Put the skewers and rice on a plate with the sweet chili sauce and serve immediately.

For chili ham, replace the pork with 10 oz cubed ham and use 1 green bell pepper, cut into wedges, instead of the lime. When threading the ham onto the skewers, alternate it with onion wedges and green pepper wedges. Serve with mango chutney instead of sweet chili sauce.

quick

chicken noodle miso soup

Serves **4**

Preparation time **15 minutes**

Cooking time **20 minutes**

sunflower oil spray

2 inch piece **fresh ginger root**, peeled and chopped

3 **garlic cloves**, crushed

pinch of **dried red pepper flakes**

3 tablespoons **miso paste**

2 tablespoons **lime juice**

7 oz **fine egg noodles**

2 **chicken breasts**, 4 oz each, finely sliced

4 oz **shiitake mushrooms**, sliced

2–3 **baby corn ears**, chopped

7 oz **sugar snap peas**, halved

2 cups **watercress**, tough stems removed

soy sauce, to serve

Heat a large saucepan, spray the bottom with oil, add the ginger, garlic, and pepper flakes and stir-fry for 1 minute. Add 7½ cups boiling water and bring to a simmer. Stir in the miso paste, lime juice, and noodles and cook for 1 minute. Cover and set aside.

Heat a large wok or skillet, spray it with oil and stir-fry the chicken, mushrooms, and corn for 2–3 minutes. Add the peas and cook for 2 minutes.

Transfer the soup to 4 bowls, spoon over the vegetables and chicken and top with watercress. Serve the soy sauce on the side.

For vegetable miso soup with shredded omelet,

omit the chicken and prepare 2 omelets using 2 eggs and 2 sliced scallions each. When the omelets are cooked, roll and shred them, then spoon over the soup with the vegetables.

fresh fava bean & herb dip

Serves **4**

Preparation time **5 minutes**,
  plus chilling

Cooking time **15 minutes**

2¼ cups fresh or frozen **fava
  beans**

1 cup **parsley**, roughly
  chopped

1 cup **cilantro**, roughly
  chopped

1–2 **green chilies**, seeded
  and chopped

2 **garlic cloves**, chopped

1½ teaspoons **ground cumin**

3 tablespoons **olive oil**

1 **onion**, thinly sliced

salt and pepper

Cook the beans in lightly salted boiling water for
5 minutes. Add the parsley and cilantro, cover, and
simmer for an additional 5 minutes. Strain and reserve
some of the cooking liquid.

Combine the beans with the chilies, garlic, cumin,
2 tablespoons oil, and 3–4 tablespoons of the reserved
cooking liquid in a food processor or blender. Process
to a smooth paste and season to taste. Add a little
more of the cooking liquid if the mixture is too dry.
Transfer to a serving dish and chill.

Heat the rest of the oil in a nonstick pan and fry the
onion briskly until golden and crisp. Spread over the
dip. If desired, serve the dip with whole-wheat pita
bread or crudités.

For eggplant dip, bake 2 foil-wrapped eggplants in a
preheated oven, 350°F, for 30–45 minutes. Mash the
flesh with 2–3 crushed garlic cloves, 2 tablespoons
olive oil, and 1 tablespoon lemon juice. Season
to taste.

broiled teriyaki bass with noodles

Serves **4**
Preparation time **5 minutes**
Cooking time **10 minutes**

sunflower oil spray
4 **bass fillets**, about 6 oz each
8 oz medium **egg noodles**
1 tablespoons **sesame oil**
2 tablespoons finely chopped
  chives
3 **scallions**, finely chopped

Teriyaki sauce
5 tablespoons **mirin** or
  medium dry sherry
5 tablespoons **light soy**
  sauce
5 tablespoons **chicken stock**

Make the teriyaki sauce. Put the mirin or sherry in a saucepan, bring to a boil, and simmer for 2 minutes or until reduced by half. Add the soy sauce and stock, stir, and remove from the heat.

Line a broiler pan with foil, spray with oil, and arrange the bass fillets on the foil. Brush the fish with the teriyaki sauce and cook under a preheated hot broiler for 5–6 minutes, basting often with the sauce.

Meanwhile, cook the noodles in lightly salted boiling water for 3 minutes or according to the instructions on the package. Drain and stir in the sesame oil, chives, and scallions.

Serve the bass on a bed of piping hot noodles and drizzle over any juices from the broiler pan.

For teriyaki tofu with stir-fried cabbage, replace the bass with 2 x 8 oz packages tofu. Slice horizontally and cook as above. Meanwhile, stir-fry 2 cups shredded Chinese cabbage and 1 sliced red bell pepper. Serve the tofu hot on a bed of the stir-fried cabbage.

marinated minty lamb kebabs

Serves **4**

Preparation time **15 minutes**, plus marinating

Cooking time **10 minutes**

1 **garlic clove**, crushed

2 tablespoons chopped **mint**

1 tablespoon ready-made **mint sauce**

⅔ cup **low-fat plain yogurt**

12 oz **lean lamb**, cubed

2 small **onions**, cut into wedges

1 **green bell pepper**, cored, seeded, and cut into wedges

lemon wedges, to serve

Mix together the garlic, mint, mint sauce, and yogurt in a medium bowl, add the lamb and stir well. Cover and allow to marinate in a cool place for 10 minutes.

Thread the lamb and onion and pepper wedges onto 8 metal skewers and cook under a preheated hot broiler for 8–10 minutes or until cooked through.

Serve the kebabs with lemon wedges and, if desired, accompany them with a green salad and couscous.

For Chinese lamb kebabs, marinate the lamb in a mixture of 2 inches fresh ginger root, peeled and finely grated, 4 tablespoons each soy sauce and dry sherry, 1 teaspoon superfine sugar, and 1 tablespoon lemon juice. Broil as above.

tuna enchiladas

Serves **4**

Preparation time **10 minutes**

Cooking time **15 minutes**

2 ripe **tomatoes**

1 **red onion**, peeled and finely
chopped

1 tablespoon **lime juice** or to
taste

8 **chapattis**

10 oz can **tuna in spring
water**, drained

1¼ cups grated **reduced-fat
cheddar cheese**

salt and pepper

fresh cilantro, chopped,
to garnish

Chop the tomatoes and mix them with the onion.
Season well and add lime juice to taste.

Spoon some of the tomato mixture over each
chapatti, top with the tuna and half the cheese. Roll
up each chapatti and arrange them in a heatproof dish.
Sprinkle with the remaining cheese and any remaining
tomato salsa.

Cover and cook in a preheated oven, 400°F, for
15 minutes until golden. Garnish with cilantro and
serve immediately.

For veggie enchiladas, slice and broil 12 mushrooms
and 2 zucchini and and use instead of the tuna. For
extra spice, add a chopped and seeded jalapeño
pepper to the tomatoes and onions.

salmon & bulghur wheat pilaf

Serves **4**
Preparation time **10 minutes**
Cooking time **10–15 minutes**

15 oz boneless, skinless
   salmon
1¼ cups **bulghur wheat**
½ cup frozen **peas**
1¼ cups chopped **runner
   beans**
2 tablespoons chopped
   chives
2 tablespoons chopped **flat
   leaf parsley**
salt and pepper

To serve
2 **lemons**, halved
low-fat yogurt

Cook the salmon in a steamer or microwave for about 10 minutes. Alternatively, wrap it in foil and cook in a preheated oven, 350°F, for 15 minutes.

Meanwhile, cook the bulghur wheat according to the instructions on the package and boil the peas and beans. Alternatively, cook the bulghur wheat, peas, and beans in the steamer with the salmon.

Flake the salmon and mix it into the bulghur wheat with the peas and beans. Fold in the chives and parsley and season to taste. Serve immediately with lemon halves and yogurt.

For ham & bulghur wheat pilaf, pan-fry 10 oz diced lean ham instead of the salmon. Replace the runner beans with the same quantity of fava beans and fold in 2 tablespoons chopped mint along with the chives and parsley.

lamb with hummus & tortillas

Serves **4**

Preparation time **30 minutes**,
    plus marinating

Cooking time **12 minutes**

1 lb **lamb loin**, cut into ¾ inch
    slices

grated zest and juice of
    1 **lemon**

1 sprig of **rosemary**, chopped

3 mixed **bell peppers**, cored,
    seeded, and chopped

1 small **eggplant**, sliced

4 flour **tortillas**

Hummus

13½ oz can **chickpeas**, rinsed
    and drained

2 tablespoons **Greek** or **whole
    milk yogurt**

2 tablespoons **lemon juice**

1 tablespoon chopped
    parsley

Put the lamb, lemon zest and juice, rosemary, and peppers in a nonmetallic bowl and stir well. Cover and allow to marinate in a cool place for 30 minutes.

Meanwhile, put the hummus ingredients in a food processor or blender and process for 30 seconds. Spoon into a bowl.

Heat a griddle or heavy skillet, add the lamb and pepper mixture and the eggplant and fry for 3—4 minutes until cooked. (You may need to do this in batches.)

Heat the tortillas according to the instructions on the package. When the lamb and vegetables are ready, wrap them in the tortillas with the hummus and serve with some arugula, if desired.

For roasted vegetables with hummus, cut the following vegetables into wedges: 1 eggplant, 1 red bell pepper, 2 zucchini, and 1 red onion. Drizzle with olive oil and sprinkle with 1 teaspoon chopped thyme. Roast in a preheated oven, 400°F, for 45 minutes. When the vegetables are tender, wrap them in warm tortillas with the hummus prepared as above.

pork with red pepper & noodles

Serves **4**
Preparation time **30 minutes**
Cooking time **10 minutes**

5 oz **flat rice noodles**
sunflower oil spray
3 **scallions**, sliced
1 **red bell pepper**, diced
2 **kaffir lime leaves**,
   shredded
2 **red chilies**, seeded
   and sliced
½ **lemon grass stalk**, finely
   chopped
1 lb **pork tenderloin**,
   shredded
2 tablespoons **soy sauce**
¾ cup **Thai fish sauce**
¼ cup **palm sugar** or **brown
   sugar**

To garnish
red basil or **basil leaves**
shredded **scallions**

Cook the noodles according to the instructions on the package.

Heat a wok or large skillet and lightly spray with oil. Add the scallions, red pepper, lime leaves, chilies, and lemon grass and stir-fry for 1 minute. Add the shredded pork and stir-fry over high heat for 2 minutes.

Add the soy sauce, fish sauce, sugar, and drained noodles and cook for about 2 minutes, using 2 spoons to lift and stir until the noodles are evenly coated and hot.

Serve immediately, garnished with basil leaves and shredded scallions.

For pork with red pepper, orange, & honey, omit the lime leaves, lemon grass stalk, fish sauce, and sugar. Stir-fry the pork as above with the scallions, red pepper, and chilies, then add the soy sauce, grated zest of 1 orange, and 3 teaspoons each fresh orange juice and honey. Add the drained noodles and cook as above. Serve garnished with orange wedges.

lemon grass fish skewers

Serves **4**
Preparation time **10 minutes**
Cooking time **5 minutes**

1 lb skinless and boneless
  haddock fillets, chopped
1 tablespoon chopped **mint**
2 tablespoons chopped
  cilantro
2 teaspoons **red Thai curry
  paste**
2 **lime leaves,** finely chopped,
  or the grated zest of 1 **lime**
2 **lemon grass stalks,**
  quartered lengthwise
sunflower oil, for brushing

To serve
ready-made **sweet chili
  sauce**
4 **lime wedges**

Put the haddock, mint, cilantro, curry paste, and
lime leaves or zest in a food processor or blender
and process for 30 seconds until well combined.

Shape the mixture into 8 portions and form each
around a lemon grass stalk "skewer."

Brush with a little oil and cook under a preheated hot
broiler for 4—5 minutes or until cooked through. Serve
with a little sweet chili sauce and lime wedges.

For rosemary swordfish skewers, replace the
haddock with 1 lb boneless swordfish, use 8 rosemary
stalks instead of the lemon grass and omit the curry
paste and cilantro. Soak the rosemary stalks in water.
Blend the swordfish with the mint and the grated
zest of 1 lemon. Season well and shape around the
rosemary stalks. Cook as above and serve with lemon
wedges. You may need to protect any exposed
rosemary stalk with foil during broiling.

bean casserole with parsley pesto

Serves **4**
Preparation time **15 minutes**
Cooking time **20 minutes**

3 oz **pancetta cubes**
1 **onion**, chopped
1 **garlic clove**, chopped
1 tablespoon chopped **thyme**
1 **carrot**, peeled and diced
13 oz can **cannellini beans**,
   drained and rinsed
13 oz can **chopped tomatoes**
¾ cup **chicken stock**
1 tablespoon **tomato paste**
½ teaspoon **powdered
   mustard**
salt and pepper
Parmesan cheese shavings,
   to serve

Parsley pesto
½ cup chopped **flat leaf
   parsley**
1 **garlic clove**, chopped
3 tablespoons **pine nuts**,
   toasted and chopped
1 tablespoon **extra virgin
   olive oil**

Heat a large, nonstick skillet and dry-fry the pancetta until it is soft. Add the onion, garlic, thyme, and carrot, then stir in the beans, tomatoes, stock, tomato paste, and powdered mustard. Season to taste and simmer for 10 minutes or until the sauce has thickened.

Meanwhile, make the pesto. Mix together the parsley, garlic, pine nuts, and oil and season to taste.

Serve the pancetta and bean mixture with the parsley pesto and Parmesan shavings.

For parsley pesto salad, simmer 1 cup long-grain rice for 12 minutes or until tender, then drain, refresh with cold water, and drain again. Mix with a 13 oz can cannellini beans, drained and rinsed, 10 halved cherry tomatoes, 1 seeded and chopped red bell pepper and the pesto.

shrimp with green leaves

Serves **4**

Preparation time **10 minutes**

Cooking time **5 minutes**

olive oil spray

20 large raw **jumbo shrimp**, with shells intact

1 **garlic clove**, chopped

4 oz **plum tomatoes**, chopped

1¼ cups **arugula**

1 cup **spinach leaves**, tough stalks removed

1¼ cups **watercress**, tough stalks removed

1 tablespoon **lemon juice**

salt and pepper

Heat a large saucepan, spray it with the oil, add the shrimp and garlic and season to taste. Cover tightly and cook, shaking the pan from time to time, for about 3 minutes or until the shrimp are cooked.

Add the tomatoes, arugula, spinach, and watercress and stir until wilted. Squeeze over the lemon juice and check the seasoning.

Serve immediately, with French bread if desired.

For garlic mushrooms with green leaves, replace the shrimp with 12 oz whole button mushrooms and cook with the garlic as above. Remove the mushrooms from the pan while you wilt the leaves and the tomatoes, then return them briefly to the pan. Serve topped with lemon zest and parsley.

chicken fajitas with tomato salsa

Serves **4**

Preparation time **15 minutes**,
  plus chilling

Cooking time **10 minutes**

1 tablespoon **olive oil**

1 large **red onion**, thinly sliced

1 **red bell pepper**, cored,
  seeded, and thinly sliced

1 **yellow bell pepper**, cored,
  seeded, and thinly sliced

1 lb skinless **chicken breasts**,
  cut into thin strips

⅛ teaspoon **paprika**

⅛ teaspoon **mild chili powder**

⅛ teaspoon **cumin**

¼ teaspoon **oregano**

4 soft flour **tortillas**

½ **iceberg lettuce**, finely
  shredded

Tomato salsa

1 small **red onion**, finely
  chopped

14 oz small **vine-ripened
  tomatoes**, chopped

2 **garlic cloves**, crushed

large handful of **cilantro
  leaves**, chopped

pepper

Make the salsa. Combine the onion, tomatoes, garlic, and cilantro in a bowl. Season with pepper, cover, and chill for 30 minutes.

Heat the oil in a wok or large nonstick skillet, add the onion and peppers and stir-fry for 3–4 minutes. Add the chicken, paprika, chili powder, cumin, and oregano and cook for an additional 5 minutes or until the chicken is cooked through.

Meanwhile, wrap the tortillas in foil and warm them in the oven for 5 minutes or according to the instructions on the package.

Spoon one-quarter of the chicken mixture into the center of each tortilla, add a couple of tablespoons of salsa and some shredded lettuce. Roll up and serve warm.

For avocado salsa, peel, pit, and finely dice 2 large ripe avocados and combine with 4 diced plum tomatoes, 1 finely chopped red onion, a 10 oz can black-eyed peas, drained and rinsed, 2 tablespoons chopped fresh cilantro, and the grated zest and juice of 1 lime.

chinese chicken with peppers

Serves **4**
Preparation time **10 minutes**
Cooking time **18 minutes**

2 inch piece **fresh ginger
   root**, grated
2 **garlic cloves**, chopped
2 **star anise**
5 tablespoons ready-made
   teriyaki marinade
3 boneless, skinless **chicken
   breasts**, diced
sunflower oil spray
½ **red bell pepper**, cored,
   seeded, and diced
½ **green bell pepper**, cored,
   seeded, and diced
½ **yellow bell pepper**, cored,
   seeded, and diced
2 **scallions**, sliced
1½ cups **easy-cook long-
   grain rice**
2½ cups **chicken stock**

Mix together the ginger, garlic, star anise, and teriyaki marinade. Add the chicken, turn to coat and set aside for 10 minutes.

Meanwhile, heat a skillet, spray it lightly with oil and cook the peppers over medium heat for 3 minutes. Add the scallions, rice, and chicken and pour over the stock. Season to taste and simmer for 15 minutes, then serve hot.

For pork with green peppers and litchis, replace the chicken with 1 lb diced pork. Replace the peppers with 1½ diced green bell peppers and stir a 13 oz can drained litchis into the pan with the onion, rice, and pork.

minted zucchini frittata

Serves **4**
Preparation time **10 minutes**
Cooking time **12–14 minutes**

4 teaspoons **olive oil**
1 **red onion**, thinly sliced
12 oz **zucchini**, diced
6 **eggs**
2 tablespoons chopped **mint**
salt and pepper

Heat the oil in a large, nonstick skillet with a flameproof handle, add the onion and zucchini and fry over gentle heat for 5 minutes or until lightly browned and just cooked.

Beat together the eggs, 2 tablespoons water, chopped mint, and a little seasoning. Add the egg mixture to the skillet. Cook, without stirring, for 4–5 minutes or until the frittata is almost set and the underside is golden brown.

Transfer the pan to a hot broiler and cook for 3–4 minutes until the top is golden and the frittata is cooked through. Cut into wedges or squares and serve with a mixed salad, if desired.

For ham, black olive, & zucchini frittata, add 7 oz diced, cooked ham and ⅛ cup halved, pitted black olives to the pan with the onion and zucchini. Cook as above and serve with a cherry tomato and basil salad on shredded leaves.

chickpea & tomato casserole

Serves **4**

Preparation time **10 minutes**

Cooking time **about 30 minutes**

3 **garlic cloves**, crushed

3 **rosemary** sprigs

2 lb **vine tomatoes**, halved

olive oil spray

1 mild **onion**, chopped

2 tablespoons **rosemary**

1 **red chili**, seeded and chopped

3 tablespoons **vegetable stock**

2 x 13½ oz cans **chickpeas**, drained and rinsed

salt and pepper

Stir the garlic and rosemary sprigs through the tomatoes. Spread them out in a roasting pan and cook in a preheated oven, 400°F, for 30 minutes.

Meanwhile, lightly spray a casserole dish with oil and gently cook the onion for 10 minutes. Add the chopped rosemary, chili, stock, and chickpeas, season to taste, cover, and transfer to the oven for 20 minutes or the remainder of the tomato cooking time.

When the tomatoes are cooked, stir them into the chickpeas with all the juices from the roasting pan. Check the seasoning and, if desired, serve with baked potatoes and a green salad.

For sausage & tomato casserole, add 4 small, sliced zucchini to the casserole dish with the onion. Broil 4 Toulouse sausages, then slice them and stir them through the casserole when you add the tomatoes. Serve with a leafy green salad.

broiled lamb with caperberries

Serves **4**

Preparation time **10 minutes**

Cooking time **10 minutes**

4 **lamb leg steaks**, about
   4 oz each, fat trimmed off

6 tablespoons chopped **flat
   leaf parsley**, plus extra
   whole sprigs to garnish

1 **garlic clove**, crushed

12 **sun-dried tomatoes**

1 tablespoon **lemon juice**

1 tablespoon **olive oil**

2 tablespoons **caperberries,**
   rinsed

salt and pepper

Season the meat and cook under a preheated hot broiler for about 5 minutes on each side until golden.

Reserve 4 tablespoons of the chopped parsley. Blend the remaining parsley with the garlic, tomatoes, lemon juice, and oil.

Spoon the tomato sauce over the lamb. Sprinkle with the reserved chopped flat leaf parsley and add the caperberries. Garnish with whole parsley sprigs and serve with pasta, if desired.

For broiled lamb with tapenade, use black olive tapenade instead of the dressing and stir all the parsley through it. To make your own tapenade, whiz 1 cup pitted black olives, 3 tablespoons extra virgin olive oil, 1 garlic clove, and 2 salted anchovies in a food processor with black pepper and add chopped flat leaf parsley to taste.

sesame tuna with spicy noodles

Serves **4**
Preparation time **10 minutes**
Cooking time **10 minutes**

10 oz **rice vermicelli noodles**
½ cup **sesame seeds**
4 **tuna steaks**, about 5 oz
  each

Chili dressing
2 **garlic cloves**, chopped
2 inch piece of **fresh ginger
  root**, peeled and grated
4 tablespoons **sweet chili
  sauce**
½ cup **cilantro leaves**, plus
  extra to garnish
2 tablespoons **oil**
1 **chili**, chopped
2 tablespoons **sesame oil**
2 tablespoons **rice vinegar**

Make the dressing by mixing together all the
ingredients. Meanwhile, cook the noodles according
to the instructions on the package and set aside.

Press the sesame seeds into both sides of the tuna.
Heat a large, heavy skillet and dry-fry the tuna for
1–2 minutes on each side, depending on the thickness,
until it is just pink in the middle.

Slice the tuna. Spoon the dressing over the hot
noodles and put the sliced tuna on top. Garnish
with cilantro leaves and serve immediately.

For sesame tofu with shiitake mushrooms,
substitute the tuna with 2 x 8 oz blocks tofu, press
in the sesame seeds and cook as above. Remove
from the pan and slice. Fry 8 oz fresh shiitake
mushrooms in the pan after the tofu and mix in
2 chopped scallions. Top the noodles with the
mushrooms and sliced tofu and serve immediately.

quick prosciutto & arugula pizza

Serves **4**
Preparation time **10 minutes**
Cooking time **10 minutes**

4 mini **pizza bases**
2 **garlic cloves**, halved
8 oz **reduced-fat mozzarella cheese**, shredded
8 **cherry tomatoes**, quartered
5 oz **prosciutto**, sliced
1¼ cups **arugula leaves**, washed
balsamic vinegar, to taste
salt and pepper

Rub the top surfaces of the pizza bases with the cut faces of the garlic cloves.

Put the pizza bases on a baking sheet, top with mozzarella and tomatoes and bake in a preheated oven, 400°F, for 10 minutes until the bread is golden.

Top the pizzas with slices of prosciutto and arugula leaves, season to taste with salt, pepper, and balsamic vinegar and serve immediately.

For tuna & pineapple pizza, drain and chop a 7½ oz can pineapple, and drain and flake a 5½ oz can tuna in spring water. Top the pizza bases with the pineapple and tuna then sprinkle with the mozzarella and tomatoes before cooking as above.

shrimp, mango, & avocado wrap

Serves **4**

Preparation time **10 minutes**, plus standing

2 tablespoons **low-fat sour cream**

2 teaspoons **tomato ketchup**

few drops of **Tabasco sauce**, to taste

10 oz cooked peeled **shrimp**

1 **mango**, peeled, pitted, and thinly sliced

1 **avocado**, peeled, pitted, and sliced

4 flour **tortillas**

2 cups **watercress**

Mix together the sour cream, ketchup, and Tabasco to taste in a bowl.

Add the shrimp, mango, and avocado and toss the mixture together.

Spoon the mixture into the tortillas, add some sprigs of watercress, roll up, and serve.

For tangy chicken wraps, marinate 10 oz chicken in a mixture of 1 tablespoon fresh lemon or lime juice, 1 tablespoon Worcestershire sauce, and 1 chopped garlic clove for 20 minutes. Cook the chicken under a preheated medium broiler for 10 minutes, turning often. Slice and use instead of the shrimp.

something
special

swordfish with couscous & salsa

Serves **4**

Preparation time **10 minutes**

Cooking time **10 minutes**

4 **swordfish steaks**, about
  5 oz each

4–5 small ripe **tomatoes**

16 Kalamata **olives** in brine,
  drained

2 tablespoons chopped **flat
  leaf parsley**

salt and pepper

1 cup **couscous**

Season the swordfish steaks with salt and pepper.

Dice or quarter the tomatoes and transfer them to a
bowl with all the juices. Remove the pits from the olives
and chop the flesh if the pieces are still large. Stir them
into the tomatoes with the parsley, season to taste and
set aside.

Cook the couscous according to the instructions on
the package and set aside.

Meanwhile, cook the swordfish steaks, 2 at a time, in
a preheated hot griddle pan. Cook on the first side for
4 minutes, without disturbing them, then turn and cook
for an additional minute.

Serve the swordfish and couscous immediately, topped
with the olive and tomato salsa and accompanied with
a green salad, if desired.

For hake with pasta & salsa, replace the couscous
with 7 oz tagliatelle or baby pasta shapes and cook
according to the package instructions. Replace the
swordfish with 4 hake fillets and cook as described
above. When the pasta is cooked, toss with the
chopped parsley and a handful of chopped capers.
Serve the hake and pasta as above, topped with
the salsa.

japanese rice with nori

Serves **4**

Preparation time **10 minutes**

Cooking time **15 minutes**

1 cup **Japanese sushi** or **glutinous rice**

2 tablespoons black or white **sesame seeds**

1 teaspoon **coarse salt**

1 tablespoon **peanut** or **vegetable oil**

2 **eggs**, beaten

4 **scallions**, finely sliced

1 **red chili**, seeded and sliced

4 tablespoons **seasoned rice vinegar**

2 teaspoons **superfine sugar**

1 tablespoon **light soy sauce**

2 pieces **pickled Japanese ginger**

2 sheets of **roasted nori** (seaweed)

Put the rice in a saucepan with 1¾ cups water. Bring to a boil, then reduce the heat and simmer, uncovered, for about 5 minutes until all the water is absorbed. Cover the pan and set aside for an additional 5 minutes, until the rice is cooked.

Meanwhile, put the sesame seeds and salt in a skillet and heat gently for about 2 minutes until the seeds are toasted. Remove and set aside.

Heat the oil in the pan, add the eggs and cook gently until just firm. Slide the omelet onto a plate, roll it up and cut it across into shreds.

Transfer the cooked rice to a bowl and stir in the scallions, chili, rice vinegar, sugar, soy sauce, ginger, and half the toasted sesame seeds. Crumble 1 sheet of nori over the rice and stir in with the omelet shreds.

Transfer to a serving dish. Crumble the remaining nori over the rice, sprinkle with the remaining toasted sesame seeds and serve immediately.

For noodle & chicken salad, replace the rice with 7 oz wheat and buckwheat noodles, cooked according to package instructions. Omit the omelet and stir-fry 8 oz shredded, cooked chicken in the oil instead.

bass with tomato & basil sauce

Serves **4**

Preparation time **10 minutes**

Cooking time **30 minutes**

8 **plum tomatoes,** halved

2 tablespoons **lemon juice**

grated zest of **1 lemon,** plus
  extra to garnish

4 **sea bass fillets,** about
  5 oz each

2 tablespoons chopped **basil**

2 tablespoons extra virgin
  olive oil

salt and pepper

To garnish

basil leaves

lemon wedges

Make the sauce up to 2 days in advance. Arrange the tomatoes in a roasting pan, season well, and cook in a preheated oven, 400°F, for 20 minutes.

Transfer the tomatoes and any cooking juices to a pan and heat through gently with the lemon juice and zest. Season to taste and set aside until ready to serve.

Season the fish fillets and cook under a preheated hot broiler for approximately 10 minutes or until the fish is cooked through.

Meanwhile, warm the sauce through. Stir the basil and oil through the sauce and spoon it over the fish. Garnish with basil leaves, more grated lemon zest, and lemon wedges.

For jumbo shrimp in tomato & basil sauce, replace the bass fillets with 16 raw and peeled jumbo shrimp. Fry the shrimp in a little oil spray until pink and cooked through. Make the sauce as above and spoon over the top of the cooked shrimp to serve.

salmon & puy lentils with parsley

Serves **4**

Preparation time **15 minutes**

Cooking time **35 minutes**

1 cup **Puy lentils**

1 **bay leaf**

1¼ cups chopped fine **green beans**

½ cup **flat leaf parsley**, chopped

2 tablespoons **Dijon mustard**

2 tablespoons **capers**, rinsed and chopped

2 tablespoons **olive oil**

2 **lemons**, finely sliced

about 1 lb **salmon fillets**

1 **fennel bulb**, finely sliced

salt and pepper

dill sprigs, to garnish

Put the lentils into a saucepan with the bay leaf and enough cold water to cover (do not add salt). Bring to a boil, reduce to a simmer, and cook for 30 minutes or until tender. Season to taste, add the beans, and simmer for 1 minute. Drain the lentils and stir in the parsley, mustard, capers, and oil. Discard the bay leaf.

Meanwhile, arrange the lemon slices on a foil-lined broiler pan and put the salmon and fennel slices on top. Season the salmon and fennel and cook under a preheated hot broiler for about 10 minutes or until the salmon is cooked through.

Serve the fennel slices and lentils with the salmon on top, garnished with dill sprigs.

For pork scallops with lentils, prepare the Puy lentils as above and replace the salmon with 4 pork scallops. Broil the pork as above, omitting the fennel. Meanwhile, finely slice 2 celery sticks and toss with a little walnut oil. Serve the lentils with the scallops on top, garnished with the celery and walnut oil.

angler fish with beans & pesto

Serves **4**

Preparation time **10 minutes**

Cooking time **10—15 minutes**

1 lb **angler fish**, cut into
    12 pieces

12 slices of **prosciutto**

12 **cherry tomatoes**

2 **yellow bell peppers**, cored,
    seeded, and cut into
    6 wedges

2 tablespoon **olive oil**

10 oz can **cannellini beans**,
    rinsed and drained

4 tablespoons **ready-made
    pesto**

Presoak 4 wooden skewers in warm water. Wrap each piece of angler fish in a slice of prosciutto. Thread these onto skewers, alternating with tomatoes and pieces of bell pepper. Brush the kebabs with the oil and cook under a preheated hot broiler for 3—4 minutes. Turn the skewers over and cook for an additional 3 minutes until cooked through.

Put the beans in a nonstick saucepan and cook, stirring, over low heat for 4—5 minutes or until hot. Stir in the pesto.

Spoon the beans onto 4 plates, top with the kebabs, and serve immediately.

For scallops with green beans & pesto, replace the angler fish with 16 scallops, wrap each one in a piece of prosciutto and skewer as above, omitting the peppers. Broil as above. Replace the cannellini beans with 8 oz green beans and cook as above. Serve immediately, with crusty French bread.

lamb stuffed with rice & peppers

Serves **4**

Preparation time **40 minutes**

Cooking time **1 hour**
   20 minutes

2 **red bell peppers**, cored,
   seeded, and halved

¼ cup **wild rice**, cooked

5 **garlic cloves**, chopped

5 **semidried tomatoes**,
   chopped

2 tablespoons chopped **flat
   leaf parsley**

1¼ lb **boneless leg of lamb**,
   butterflied

salt and pepper

4 **artichoke halves**

Put the pepper halves in a roasting pan and cook in a preheated oven, 350°F, for 20 minutes, until the skin has blackened and blistered. Cover with damp paper towels and set aside. When the peppers are cool enough to handle, peel off the skin and chop the flesh. (Leave the oven on.)

Mix together one of the chopped peppers, the rice, garlic, tomatoes, and parsley. Season to taste.

Put the lamb on a board and make a horizontal incision, almost all the way along, to make a cavity for stuffing. Fold back the top half, spoon in the stuffing and fold back the top. Secure with skewers.

Cook the lamb for 1 hour, basting frequently and adding the artichokes and other pepper for the last 15 minutes of cooking time. Slice the lamb and serve immediately with roasted new potatoes, if desired.

For lamb stuffed with cilantro & mint, combine the grated zest and juice of 1 lime, 2 finely chopped scallions, 2 tablespoons each chopped cilantro and chopped mint, 2 tablespoons olive oil, 2 finely chopped garlic cloves, and season. Spoon over the lamb, roll and skewer, then roast as above.

sesame & ginger wraps

Serves **4**
Preparation time **15 minutes**
Cooking time **5–10 minutes**

Sesame and ginger sauce
1 **garlic clove**, chopped
2 inch piece **fresh ginger root**, peeled and roughly chopped
3 tablespoons **light brown sugar**
4 teaspoons **soy sauce**
5 teaspoons **wine** or **rice vinegar**
2 tablespoons **tomato paste**
2 tablespoons **sesame seeds**, plus extra to garnish

Pancakes
8 **rice pancakes**
2 **carrots**
1½ cups **bean sprouts** or mixed **sprouting beans**
small handful of **mint**, roughly chopped
1 **celery stick**, thinly sliced
4 **scallions**, thinly sliced diagonally
1 tablespoon **soy sauce**

Put all the ingredients for the sauce, except the sesame seeds, in a food processor or blender and process to a thin paste. Alternatively, crush the garlic, and grate the ginger and beat into the remaining ingredients. Stir in the sesame seeds and transfer to a serving bowl.

Soften the rice pancakes according to the instructions on the package. Cut the carrots into fine shreds and mix with the bean sprouts or sprouting beans, mint, celery, scallions, and soy sauce.

Spoon the vegetable mixture into the center of each pancake. Fold in the bottom edge of each to the middle, then roll up from one side to the other to form a pocket.

Steam the pancakes for about 5 minutes until they are heated through. Alternatively, place them on a wire rack set over a roasting pan of boiling water and cover with foil. Serve immediately with the sauce and garnished with extra sesame seeds.

For veggie pancakes with plum & wasabi sauce, cook 8 oz pitted and chopped ripe red plums in a saucepan, covered, with 2 tablespoons water until soft. Puree with 1 tablespoon soy sauce then add wasabi sauce and superfine sugar to taste. Make the pancakes as above and serve drizzled with the plum and wasabi sauce.

lime & chili marinated chicken

Serves **4**
Preparation time **15–20
minutes**, plus marinating
Cooking time **10 minutes**

4 boneless, skinless **chicken
breasts**, about 4 oz each
4 **limes**
2 **garlic cloves**, chopped
2 tablespoons chopped **dried
or fresh red chili**
3 tablespoons **sunflower oil**
7 oz **rice noodles**
2 tablespoons chopped
cilantro, to garnish
salt and pepper

Presoak about 12 wooden skewers in warm water.
Cut the chicken into strips.

Grate the zest and squeeze the juice from 2 limes and
mix with the garlic, chili, and oil. Toss the chicken in the
lime and chili mix, season with salt and pepper, and set
aside for 1 hour.

Thread pieces of chicken onto skewers, not
overloading each one. Halve the remaining limes. Cook
the chicken and lime halves under a preheated hot
broiler or on a preheated griddle for about 10 minutes.

Meanwhile, cook the noodles according to the
instructions on the package.

Serve the chicken with the noodles, garnished with
cilantro, and the caramelized lime halves.

For chicken tikka, finely chop 1 onion, 1 large
seeded chili, a ¾ inch piece fresh ginger root and
2 finely chopped garlic cloves. Combine with ⅔ cup
low-fat plain yogurt, 3 teaspoons mild curry paste, and
4 tablespoons chopped fresh cilantro. Marinate the
chicken, then broil and serve as above.

lamb loin with vegetables

Serves **4**

Preparation time **20 minutes**

Cooking time **35—45 minutes**

1 lb even-size baby **new potatoes**

1 tablespoon chopped **rosemary**

13 oz **lamb loin**, diced

3 **garlic cloves**, halved

12½ oz can **artichokes**, drained, rinsed, and halved

1 **red bell pepper**, seeded and quartered

7 oz small **leeks**

salt and pepper

Put the potatoes in a pan with plenty of lightly salted water and bring to a boil. Drain immediately and toss with the rosemary.

Transfer the potatoes to a roasting pan with the lamb, garlic, artichokes, and peppers. Cover and cook in a preheated oven, 350°F, for 30—40 minutes or until cooked through and the potato skins are golden. Meanwhile, steam the leeks.

Drain the excess fat and serve the lamb with the roasted vegetables, leeks, and any pan juices.

For herby baked lamb, before baking sprinkle the diced lamb with 6—8 tablespoons lemon juice, ¼ teaspoon each dried oregano and thyme, the leaves torn from 2 oregano sprigs, 4 lemon thyme sprigs, and salt and pepper.

pork with soy-garlic marinade

Serves **4**
Preparation time **5 minutes**,
 plus marinating
Cooking time **20 minutes**

2 **pork tenderloins**, 8 oz each
1 tablespoon **flax seeds**
⅔ cup **dry white wine**

Soy and garlic marinade
1 **cinnamon stick**
2 tablespoons **soy sauce**
2 **garlic cloves**, crushed
1 teaspoon grated **fresh
 ginger root**
1 tablespoon **honey**
1 teaspoon crushed **coriander
 seeds**
1 teaspoon **sesame oil**

Mix together the ingredients for the marinade. Put the pork in a shallow, nonmetallic dish, cover evenly with the marinade, and leave for at least 2–3 hours, preferably overnight.

Drain the pork, reserving the marinade. Press the flax seeds into the pork so that both sides of each tenderloin are evenly covered.

Heat an ovenproof skillet over a high heat on the burner. Seal the pork and transfer it to a preheated oven, 350°F. Cook for 18–20 minutes or until golden brown.

Meanwhile, remove the cinnamon stick from the marinade and pour the liquid into a nonstick pan. Add the wine and bring to a boil. Reduce the heat and simmer until it has the consistency of a sticky glaze. Remove from the heat and set aside.

Remove the pork from the oven and cut it into ¼ inch slices. Serve on a bed of steamed vegetables, such as pak choi or spinach, and drizzle the glaze over the pork.

For pork with orange marinade, mix the grated zest of 1 orange with 3 crushed garlic cloves, the crushed seeds from 8 cardamom pods, and a little salt and pepper. Marinate and cook the pork as above.

shrimp with lemon & tomato

Serves **4**
Preparation time **10 minutes**
Cooking time **30–40 minutes**

olive oil spray
1 **onion**, chopped
2 **garlic cloves**, finely
  chopped
1 **carrot**, finely chopped
1 **celery stick**, finely chopped
2 tablespoons **white wine**
13 oz can **chopped tomatoes**
10 oz raw **jumbo shrimp**,
  shells removed
grated zest of 1 **lemon**
1½ lb **new potatoes**, cut into
  even sizes
1 tablespoon **olive oil**
1¼ cups **arugula**, to garnish
salt and pepper

Lightly spray a medium saucepan with oil, add the onion, garlic, carrot, and celery and cook gently for about 15 minutes or until soft. (Add a few drops of water if the pan gets too dry.) Increase the heat and stir in the wine. Add the tomatoes, reduce to a simmer, and cook for 10 minutes until the sauce is smooth and thick.

Add the shrimp and simmer for 3–4 minutes or until the shrimp are just cooked. Stir in half the lemon zest.

Meanwhile, steam the potatoes, then toss them in the remaining lemon zest, pepper, and oil. Serve them with the shrimp, garnished with arugula.

For smoked haddock & eggs with lemon & tomato, poach 13 oz smoked haddock instead of the shrimp. Cook the tomato sauce as above and stir through 4 hard-cooked and quartered eggs with the haddock. Serve with cooked pasta and garnish with a handful of parsley.

chicken with pesto & polenta

Serves **4**
Preparation time **15 minutes**
Cooking time **10 minutes**

4 **chicken breasts**, about
  4 oz each
½ cup **basil leaves**
2 tablespoons **olive oil**
2 tablespoons **pine nuts**,
  toasted
1 **garlic clove**, peeled
2 tablespoons grated
  Parmesan cheese
½ cup **arugula leaves**
1¼ cups instant **polenta**
salt and pepper

Slice the chicken breasts horizontally through the middle and season all 8 pieces.

Put the basil, oil, pine nuts, garlic, Parmesan, and arugula together in a food processor or blender and process until finely chopped. Set aside.

Cook the chicken under a preheated hot broiler for 5–7 minutes until just cooked through and still succulent.

Meanwhile, stir the polenta into 3½ cups lightly salted boiling water and keep stirring for about 2 minutes while it cooks. Stir the arugula pesto through the polenta.

Serve the chicken slices on top of the polenta.

For chicken with mixed vegetable mash, replace the polenta with 1 lb potatoes and 8 oz each rutabaga and carrots. Boil the vegetables for 12–15 minutes until soft then mash to a creamy consistency. Swirl the arugula pesto through the mash.

yellow split pea & pepper patties

Serves **4**
Preparation time **10–15**
 minutes, plus chilling
Cooking time **40–50 minutes**

3 **garlic cloves**
1 cup **yellow split peas**
3 cups **vegetable stock**
olive oil spray
2 **red bell peppers**, halved
 and seeded
1 **yellow bell pepper**, halved
 and seeded
1 **red onion**, quartered
1 tablespoon chopped **mint**
2 tablespoons **capers**, rinsed
 and chopped
flour, for dusting
salt and pepper
ready-made **tzatziki** or **raita**,
 to serve

Peel and halve a garlic clove and cook it with the split peas in the stock for 40 minutes. Check the seasoning and allow to cool slightly.

Meanwhile, lightly spray a roasting pan with oil. Put the remaining garlic cloves in the pan with the peppers and onion and cook in a preheated oven, 400°F, for 20 minutes. Squeeze the roasted garlic cloves from their skins and chop with the roasted vegetables.

Mix the split peas with the roasted vegetables, mint, and capers. Flour your hands and shape the mixture into patties. Refrigerate until ready to cook.

Heat a skillet and spray with oil. Cook the patties, in batches if necessary, allowing them to cook undisturbed for 2 minutes on each side. Serve either hot or cold, garnished with mint leaves, with tzatziki or raita on the side.

For homemade tzatziki, finely chop ½ cucumber and combine with 1 pressed garlic clove, 2 tablespoons chopped fresh mint and 1¼ cups yogurt.

chicken with paprika & red wine

Serves **4**

Preparation time **15 minutes**

Cooking time **30–40 minutes**

1 **garlic bulb**

1¼ lb **new potatoes**

1 tablespoon chopped
  rosemary

2 tablespoons **olive oil**

4 boneless, skinless **chicken
  breasts**, about 5 oz each,
  diced

1 mild **Spanish onion,**
  chopped

1 **red bell pepper**, cored,
  seeded, and chopped

1 **bay leaf**

3 **thyme** sprigs

1 tablespoon **smoked
  paprika** (pimentón)

1¾ cups **red wine**

1 cup **chicken stock**

salt and pepper

Roast the whole garlic bulb in a preheated oven,
400°F, for 30 minutes. At the same time, roast the
potatoes for 30 minutes with a little rosemary and salt.

Heat the oil in a saucepan and cook the chicken until
golden. Add the onion, bell pepper, bay leaf, thyme, and
smoked paprika, season to taste, and cook, stirring
frequently, until the vegetables are soft. Add the wine
and stock and cook for 20 minutes to reduce.

Squeeze the soft pulp from the cooked garlic and
add it to the chicken to taste. Season with more
pepper if necessary.

Remove the bay leaf and thyme and serve the chicken
with the roast potatoes and, if desired, baby zucchini
and carrots or shredded green cabbage.

For pancetta & mushroom in red wine, replace the
chicken with 7 oz diced pancetta or bacon. Continue
as above, omitting the roasted garlic. Simmer and add
7 oz halved mushrooms 5 minutes before the end of
cooking. Serve as above.

beef with red pepper crust

Serves **4**

Preparation time **15 minutes**

Cooking time **about 30 minutes**

1 **red bell pepper**, halved and seeded

2 **garlic cloves**

8 dry **black olives**, pitted

2 teaspoons **olive oil**

2 teaspoons **capers**

8 **shallots**, peeled

3 tablespoons **balsamic vinegar**

1 teaspoon **light brown sugar**

4 **beef tenderloin steaks**, about 4 oz each

salt and pepper

Cook the pepper under a preheated hot broiler until the skin blackens. Remove and cover with damp paper towels until it is cool enough to handle, then peel and chop.

Blend together the garlic, olives, 1 teaspoon oil, the capers, and the chopped red pepper.

Put the shallots and the remaining oil in a small pan. Cover and cook, stirring frequently, over low heat for 15 minutes. Add the vinegar and sugar and cook uncovered, stirring frequently, for an additional 5 minutes.

Season the steaks and cook, 2 at a time, in a preheated heavy skillet or griddle pan. Cook on one side, then transfer to a baking sheet. Top each steak with some red pepper mix. Bake in a preheated oven, 400°F, for 5 minutes or according to taste. Allow to stand in a warm place for 5 minutes before serving with the balsamic shallots and, if desired, steamed wholegrain rice.

For beef tenderloin with mushroom crust, blend 12 oz chopped mushrooms with 2 crushed garlic cloves, 1 chopped onion, 2 teaspoons olive oil, and seasoning. Cook as above for 10 minutes or until reduced down to concentrate. Add juice of ½ lemon, 2 tablespoons chopped fresh parsley, and a dash of brandy, then cook for an additional 5 minutes. Cook the steaks as above and top with the mushroom mixture.

pork with fennel & pepper

Serves **4**

Preparation time **20 minutes**

Cooking time **1 hour**

2 **garlic cloves**, sliced

2 teaspoon **light brown sugar**

2 tablespoons **balsamic vinegar**

1 lb **pork tenderloin**

1 **red bell pepper**, cored, seeded, and cut into 8 wedges

2 **fennel bulbs**, finely sliced

3 tablespoons **chicken stock**

1 tablespoon **olive oil**

7 oz **broccoli**, sliced

8 **semidried tomato quarters**

salt and pepper

Mix together the garlic, sugar, and vinegar, and season to taste. Put the pork in a nonmetallic dish, pour over the marinade and set aside while you prepare the vegetables.

Put together in a roasting pan the bell pepper, fennel, stock, and oil. Add salt and pepper and cook in a preheated oven, 400°F, for 40 minutes.

Drain the pork (discard the marinade), add it to the vegetables in the roasting pan and cook for 20 minutes or until it is just cooked and golden and the juices run clear. Add the broccoli and tomatoes for the last 10 minutes of cooking time.

Slice the pork, arrange the fennel, broccoli, and red pepper over the slices and spoon over any pan juices. Serve with basmati and wild rice, if desired.

For creamy sweet potato mash, to serve as an accompaniment, boil 2 lb sweet potatoes for 12 minutes or until soft. Mash with ½ cup low-fat cream cheese and add a handful of chopped chives and a pinch of cinnamon.

indonesian shrimp salad

Serves **4**

Preparation time **20 minutes**

Cooking time **5 minutes**

4 oz **rice noodles**

½ cup thinly sliced **cucumber**

2 tablespoons **rice vinegar**

2 tablespoons **superfine sugar**

1 **egg**, beaten

oil spray

4 **shallots**, sliced

2 **garlic cloves**, crushed

1 teaspoon grated **fresh ginger root**

1 teaspoon **ground coriander**

2 **bell peppers**, chopped

3 **red chilies**, sliced

1 tablespoon **Thai fish sauce**

8 oz cooked peeled **shrimp**

1 tablespoon **soy sauce**

salt

To serve

cilantro leaves

3 tablespoons chopped roasted **peanuts**

2 **scallions**, finely sliced

shrimp crackers

Cook the noodles according to the instructions on the package. Drain, rinse well, and set aside.

Pickle the cucumber in equal quantities of rice vinegar and sugar for 5 minutes, drain and set aside.

Mix the egg with 3 tablespoons water. Spray a wok or large skillet with oil and, when it is quite hot, make a thin omelet with the egg mixture. Roll it up, allow to cool, and cut into thin strips.

Combine the shallots, garlic, ginger, and ground coriander in a large bowl. Add the peppers, chilies, fish sauce, shrimp, and noodles and mix in, using 2 spoons to lift and stir, until they are thoroughly combined. Add the soy sauce and salt to taste.

Transfer to a serving dish and serve with the omelet strips, pickled cucumber, cilantro leaves, peanuts, and scallions, and with shrimp crackers on the side.

For hot & sweet pork with rice, cook 1¼ cups rice according to the package instructions, instead of the noodles. Meanwhile, stir-fry 8 oz lean boneless pork strips until cooked, then mix with the hot rice and dressed shrimp. Garnish with the omelet and pickled cucumber, as above.

tamarind & lemon grass beef

Serves **4**
Preparation time **15 minutes**
Cooking time **12 minutes**

1 tablespoon **oil**
1 lb lean **beef**, cut into strips
2 **lemon grass stalks**,
   chopped
6 **shallots**, chopped
2 **green chilies**, chopped
3 tablespoons **tamarind
   paste**
2 tablespoons **lime juice**
2 teaspoons **Thai fish sauce**
2 teaspoons **brown sugar**
1 cup shredded **green
   papaya**

Heat the oil in a wok or skillet, toss in the meat, and
cook over a high heat for 2–3 minutes.

Add the lemon grass, shallots, and chilies and stir-
fry for an additional 5 minutes or until the meat is
well browned.

Add the tamarind paste, lime juice, fish sauce, sugar,
and papaya and stir-fry for an additional 4 minutes.

Serve immediately, if desired with coconut rice and
a salad.

For tofu with tamarind & lemon grass, proceed
as above but replace the beef with 8 oz tofu, drained
and sliced. Stir-fry 4 oz each snow peas and sliced
shiitake mushrooms in place of the papaya and
replace the fish sauce with soy sauce.

vegetarian

chickpea & tomato soup

Serves **4**

Preparation time **15 minutes**

Cooking time **10 minutes**

1 tablespoon **olive oil**

1 **onion**, roughly chopped

1 **garlic clove**, crushed

1 **carrot**, roughly chopped

1 **red bell pepper**, cored, seeded, and roughly chopped

1 teaspoon **cumin seeds**

2 cups hot **vegetable stock**

13 oz can **chopped tomatoes**

13½ oz can **chickpeas**, drained and rinsed

2 tablespoons each **pumpkin, sesame, and sunflower seeds**

2 tablespoons chopped **cilantro**

salt and pepper

Heat the oil in a large saucepan over medium heat, add the onion, garlic, carrot, bell pepper, and cumin seeds and stir-fry for about 1 minute. Add the stock and tomatoes and simmer for 5 minutes until the vegetables are soft.

Meanwhile, dry-fry the garnish seeds in a pan over medium heat until they are golden. Set aside to cool.

Remove the vegetable pan from the heat and use a hand-held blender to puree the vegetables. Alternatively, mash them by hand. Stir through the chickpeas and heat through for 2 minutes.

Season to taste, sprinkle with the roasted seeds and fresh cilantro and serve with crusty mixed grain bread, if desired.

For tomato & pepper casserole, halve the amount of stock and cook the vegetables as above, but do not blend. Prepare 1½ cups couscous by pouring over boiling water to a depth of 1 inch. Allow to stand for a few minutes before separating the grains with a fork and serving with the casserole.

carrot & chickpea soup

Serves **4**
Preparation time **25 minutes**
Cooking time **about 40 minutes**

1 tablespoon **sunflower oil**
1 large **onion**, chopped
1 lb **carrots**, diced
1 teaspoon **ground cumin**
1 teaspoon **fennel seeds**, roughly crushed
¾ inch **fresh ginger root**, peeled and finely chopped
1 **garlic clove**, finely chopped
13½ oz can **chickpeas**, drained
5 cups **vegetable stock**
1¼ cups **lowfat milk**
salt and pepper

To garnish
1 teaspoon **sunflower oil**
½ cup **slivered almonds**
pinch of ground **cumin**
pinch of **paprika**

Heat the oil in a saucepan, add the onion and fry gently, stirring, for 5 minutes or until lightly browned. Mix in the carrots, ground spices, ginger, and garlic and cook for 1 minute.

Mix in the chickpeas, stock, and a little seasoning, bring to a boil, cover, and simmer for 30 minutes or until the vegetables are tender.

Puree the soup in batches until smooth, in a food processor or blender, then return to the pan and stir in the milk. Reheat gently.

Meanwhile, make the garnish. Heat the oil in a small skillet, add the almonds, cumin, and paprika and cook for 2–3 minutes until golden brown.

Ladle the soup into bowls and top with the almonds, cumin, and paprika. Serve with warm bread, if desired.

For carrot & lentil soup, substitute the chickpeas with a 13½ oz can green lentils. You can also use cannellini beans or other canned legumes. Omit the milk, but add an extra 1¼ cups stock. Otherwise, proceed as above. Serve the soup, then swirl 1 teaspoon Greek or whole milk yogurt through each bowl.

gazpacho

Serves **4**

Preparation time **15 minutes**, plus chilling

Cooking time **25 minutes**

1½ lb ripe **tomatoes**

1 large **fennel bulb**

¾ teaspoon **coriander seeds**

½ teaspoon **mixed peppercorns**

1 tablespoon **extra virgin olive oil**

1 large **garlic clove**, crushed

1 small **onion**, chopped

1 tablespoon **balsamic vinegar**

1 tablespoon **lemon juice**

1 tablespoon chopped **oregano**

1 teaspoon **tomato paste**

1 rounded teaspoon **rock salt**

green olives, finely sliced, to garnish

Put the tomatoes in a large pan or bowl and pour over enough boiling water to cover. Leave for about 1 minute, then drain, skin carefully, and roughly chop the flesh.

Trim the green fronds from the fennel and discard. Finely slice the bulb and put it in a saucepan with 1¼ cups lightly salted boiling water. Cover and simmer for 10 minutes.

Meanwhile, crush the coriander seeds and peppercorns using a mortar and pestle. Gently heat the oil in a large pan and add the crushed spices, garlic, and onion. Cook gently for 5 minutes.

Add the vinegar, lemon juice, tomatoes, and oregano, reserving a few oregano leaves to garnish. Give the mixture a good stir and add the fennel along with the cooking liquid, tomato paste, and salt. Bring to a simmer and allow to cook, uncovered, for 10 minutes.

Transfer the soup to a food processor or blender and process lightly. Cool and chill overnight and serve garnished with the reserved oregano leaves and green olives.

For easy almond gazpacho, blend together in a food processor 2 cups ground almonds, 3 cups ice water, 1½ cups bread crumbs, 2 crushed garlic cloves, 3 tablespoons olive oil, a splash of white wine vinegar, and seasoning. Chill for one hour and check seasoning again before serving.

roasted pepper & tomato soup

Serves **4**
Preparation time **10 minutes**
Cooking time **40 minutes**

4 **red bell peppers**, cored
 and seeded
1 lb **tomatoes**, halved
1 teaspoon **olive oil**
1 **onion**, chopped
1 **carrot**, chopped
2½ cups **vegetable stock**
2 tablespoons **low-fat sour
 cream**
handful of **basil leaves**, torn
pepper

Put the peppers, skin side up, and the tomatoes, skin side down, on a baking sheet under a hot broiler and cook for 8–10 minutes until the skins of the peppers are blackened. Cover the peppers with damp paper towels, allow to cool, then remove the skins and slice the flesh. Allow the tomatoes to cool, then remove the skins.

Heat the oil in a large saucepan, add the onion and carrot and fry for 5 minutes. Add the stock and the skinned roasted peppers and tomatoes, bring to a boil, and simmer for 20 minutes until the carrot is tender.

Transfer the soup to a food processor or blender and process until smooth, in batches if necessary. Return to the pan and heat through gently. Stir through the sour cream and basil, season well with pepper and serve.

For roasted zucchini & pea soup, replace the bell peppers with 4 medium zucchini, sliced lengthwise and roasted as above. Add 1⅓ cups frozen peas with the stock and bring to a boil. Check for seasoning and garnish with torn basil and mint.

chickpea & parsley soup

Serves **6**
Preparation time **15 minutes**,
  plus soaking
Cooking time **30 minutes**

1 small **onion**
3 **garlic cloves**
¾ cup **parsley**
2 tablespoons **olive oil**
13½ oz can **chickpeas**,
  drained and rinsed
5 cups **vegetable stock**
grated zest and juice of
  ½ **lemon**
salt and pepper

Put the onion, garlic, and parsley in a food processor or blender and process until finely chopped.

Heat the oil in a saucepan and cook the onion mixture over a low heat until slightly softened. Add the chickpeas and cook gently for 1–2 minutes.

Add the stock, season well with salt and pepper and bring to a boil. Cover and cook for 20 minutes or until the chickpeas are really tender.

Allow the soup to cool for a while, then partly puree it in a food processor or blender or mash it with a fork so that it retains plenty of texture.

Pour the soup into a clean pan, add the lemon juice, and adjust the seasoning if necessary. Heat through gently. Serve the soup topped with grated lemon zest and cracked black pepper.

For flageolet, cannellini, & parsley soup, replace the chickpeas with ¾ cup each canned flageolet and cannellini beans, and use the zest and juice of 1 lemon. Otherwise, cook as above.

pea & lettuce soup with croutons

Serves **4**
Preparation time **10 minutes**
Cooking time **25–30 minutes**

2 tablespoons **butter**
1 large **onion**, finely chopped
3 cups frozen **peas**
2 small crisphead **lettuces**,
   roughly chopped
4 cups **vegetable stock**
grated zest and juice of
   ½ **lemon**
salt and pepper

Sesame croutons
2 thick slices of **bread,** cubed
1 tablespoon **olive oil**
1 tablespoon **sesame seeds**

Make the croutons. Brush the bread cubes with the oil and put them in a roasting pan. Sprinkle with the sesame seeds and cook in a preheated oven, 400°F, for 10 minutes or until golden.

Meanwhile, heat the butter in a large saucepan, add the onion and cook for 5 minutes or until beginning to soften. Add the peas, lettuces, stock, lemon zest and juice, and seasoning. Bring to a boil, reduce the heat, cover, and simmer for 10 minutes.

Allow the soup to cool slightly, then transfer to a food processor or blender and process until smooth. Return the soup to the pan, adjust the seasoning if necessary and heat through gently.

Spoon the soup into warm serving bowls and serve sprinkled with the croutons.

For minted pea & watercress soup, replace the lettuce with 2 cups watercress, torn into pieces. Cook the watercress as for lettuce, simmering for 10 minutes but omitting the lemon zest and juice. When returning the soup to the pan after processing, add 2 tablespoons chopped mint leaves.

spicy goan eggplant curry

Serves **4**

Preparation time **15 minutes**

Cooking time **20 minutes**

1 teaspoon **cayenne pepper**

2 fresh **green chilies**, seeded and sliced

½ teaspoon **turmeric**

4 **garlic cloves**, crushed

1 inch piece of **fresh ginger root**, peeled and grated

1 teaspoon **cumin seeds**, toasted

4 teaspoons **coriander seeds**, toasted

13 oz can **coconut milk**

1 tablespoon **tamarind paste**

1 large **eggplant**, thinly sliced lengthwise

salt and pepper

Mix together the cayenne, chilies, turmeric, garlic, and ginger with 1¼ cups warm water.

Crush the cumin and coriander seeds together, add them to the sauce and simmer for 10 minutes until thickened. Season to taste. Stir in the coconut milk and tamarind paste.

Arrange the eggplant slices in a foil-lined broiler pan and brush the tops with some of the curry sauce. Cook under a preheated hot broiler until golden.

Serve the eggplant slices in the curry sauce and, if desired, with naan bread or chapattis.

For cashew nut curry, add 1½ cups roasted cashew nuts to the curry sauce. To roast, soak in water for 20 minutes, chop, then heat in a dry pan shaking regularly until lightly browned. Replace the eggplant with 4 sliced zucchini and broil as above. Drizzle with walnut oil and season well.

red rice & pumpkin risotto

Serves **4**
Preparation time **20 minutes**
Cooking time **35 minutes**

4 cups **vegetable stock**
1¼ cups **Camargue red rice**
1 tablespoon **olive oil**
1 **onion**, finely chopped
2 **garlic cloves**, finely
   chopped
1½ lb **pumpkin**, peeled,
   seeded, and diced
5 tablespoons finely chopped
   fresh basil or **oregano**, plus
   extra leaves to garnish
2 oz **Parmesan cheese**,
   coarsely grated, plus
   shavings to garnish
salt and pepper

Put the stock in a large saucepan, add the rice, and simmer for 35 minutes.

Meanwhile, heat the oil in a skillet, add the onion and cook, stirring occasionally, for 5 minutes or until softened. Add the garlic, pumpkin, and a little salt and pepper, mix together, then cover and cook over moderate heat for 10 minutes, stirring occasionally.

Drain the rice and reserve the cooking liquid. Stir the chopped herbs into the skillet with the drained rice and grated Parmesan. Adjust the seasoning and moisten with the reserved rice liquid if necessary.

Spoon into shallow dishes and serve garnished with extra herbs and Parmesan shavings.

For crunchy cabbage salad, to serve as an accompaniment, blanch 8 oz crisp green beans. Finely shred ¼ red cabbage and a handful fresh chopped parsley. Mix the beans, cabbage, and parsley, then drizzle with walnut oil.

roasted pumpkin with feta

Serves **4**

Preparation time **10 minutes**

Cooking time **40 minutes**

1¼ lb **pumpkin** or **butternut squash**, cut into 2 inch wedges

2 tablespoons **olive oil**

1 tablespoon **lemon juice**

2 tablespoons chopped **mint**, plus shredded **mint** to garnish

7 oz **feta cheese**

½ cup **walnuts**, chopped

8 **sun-dried tomatoes**, chopped

2 cups **baby spinach leaves**

salt and pepper

Toss the pumpkin pieces in 1 tablespoon oil, season, and spread out in a roasting pan. Roast in a preheated oven, 400°F, for 30 minutes.

Mix the remaining oil with the lemon juice and mint. Spoon the mixture over the feta cheese and set aside.

Add the walnuts and the tomatoes to the pumpkin and bake for an additional 10 minutes.

Serve the pumpkin with the walnuts and tomatoes and any pan juices. Crumble over the cheese and pour over the marinade. Serve with the spinach leaves and garnished with shredded mint.

For roasted pumpkin with Stilton, walnuts, & black olives, replace the tomatoes with 16 roughly chopped black olives. Replace the feta with the same quantity of Stilton and serve the salad with arugula leaves.

vegetable gratin with herby crust

Serves **4**

Preparation time **20 minutes**

Cooking time **45 minutes**

¼ cup **reduced-fat sunflower spread**

13 oz waxy **potatoes**, peeled and sliced

7 oz **sweet potato**, peeled and sliced

7 oz **carrots**, sliced

2 **garlic cloves**, chopped

1¼ cups **half-fat sour cream**

1 cup **vegetable stock**

1 tablespoon grated **Parmesan cheese**

2 tablespoons chopped **sage**

1 tablespoon chopped **rosemary**

1½ cups **bread crumbs**

salt and pepper

Lightly grease a square ovenproof dish with the sunflower spread. Layer the sliced vegetables in the dish, adding a little garlic and seasoning between each layer.

Heat the sour cream with the stock and pour it over the vegetables.

Mix together the Parmesan, sage, rosemary, and bread crumbs, season, and sprinkle over the vegetables. Bake in a preheated oven, 400°F, for 45 minutes until golden and cooked through. Serve immediately.

For beet gratin with nutty crust, replace the carrot with 8 oz sliced beet and cook as above. When preparing the topping, add ⅔ cup chopped pecans. Serve with a shredded red cabbage salad.

dhal patties with yogurt relish

Serves **4**

Preparation time **30 minutes**, plus chilling

Cooking time **20 minutes**

2 x 13½ oz cans **green lentils**, drained and rinsed

2 cups **vegetable stock**

1 **bay leaf**

2 inch **cinnamon stick**

2 **cardamom pods**

2 tablespoons chopped **cilantro**

2 tablespoons chopped **mint**

1 **red onion**, finely sliced

1 cup **nonfat yogurt**

1⅔ cups frozen **peas**

4 tablespoons **dhansak curry paste**, or to taste

sunflower oil spray

salt and pepper

Presoak some 6 inch wooden skewers in warm water. Combine the lentils with the stock, bay leaf, cinnamon stick, and cardamom pods in a pan, season with salt, and simmer for 10 minutes or until the lentils are soft.

Meanwhile, to make the yogurt relish, mix together the cilantro, mint, onion, and yogurt and add salt and pepper to taste.

Cook the peas in boiling water. Drain the lentils and remove the bay leaf, cinnamon stick, and cardamom pods. Transfer the peas and lentils to a food processor or blender and process briefly. Stir the pea mixture into the curry paste and use 2 teaspoons to shape the mixture into small balls. Refrigerate until ready to cook.

Put 3–4 balls on each skewer. Heat a skillet and spray it with oil. Fry the skewers (in batches if necessary) over medium heat for 2 minutes undisturbed, then turn and cook the other side. Serve hot with the yogurt relish.

For cucumber raita, slice, salt, and drain 1 cucumber to remove the excess water, then combine it with ½ teaspoon each ground cumin and salt, 1 teaspoon each sugar and lemon juice, and the nonfat yogurt.

stilton & leek tartlets

Serves **4**
Preparation time **15 minutes**
Cooking time **25 minutes**

1 teaspoon **olive oil**
8 small **leeks**, finely sliced
2 oz **Stilton cheese**, crumbled
1 teaspoon chopped **thyme**
2 **eggs**, beaten
4 tablespoons **low-fat sour cream**
12 x 6 inch squares **phyllo pastry**
milk, for brushing

Heat the oil in a saucepan, add the leeks and fry for 3–4 minutes until softened.

Stir half the Stilton and the thyme into the leek mixture, then blend together the remaining Stilton, the eggs, and sour cream in a bowl.

Brush the phyllo squares with a little milk and use them to line 4 fluted tart pans, each 4 inches across. Spoon the leek mixture into the pans, then pour over the cheese and egg mixture.

Place the pans on a baking sheet and bake in a preheated oven, 400°F, for 15–20 minutes until the filling is set.

For scallion & cheddar tartlets, use the same quantity of mature cheddar cheese instead of Stilton and grate it coarsely. Slice 2 bunches of large scallions and fry for 1 minute, then remove from the heat. Add the scallions and continue as above.

pilaf with nuts, lemon, & herbs

Serves **4**

Preparation time **15 minutes**

Cooking time **10 minutes**

2 tablespoons **olive oil**

1 **mild onion**, chopped

2 **garlic cloves**, crushed

1¼ cups **vegetable stock**

3 cups **couscous**

1 **pomegranate**

⅓ cup **pine nuts**, toasted

3 tablespoons chopped **flat leaf parsley**

3 tablespoons chopped **dill**

3 tablespoons chopped **cilantro**

grated zest and juice of

1 **lemon**

salt and pepper

Heat the oil in a large skillet and cook the onion and garlic for about 5 minutes or until soft. Add the stock and heat, then add the couscous. Stir, cover, and allow to steam over gentle heat for 5 minutes.

Meanwhile, take the seeds from the pomegranate, working over a bowl to catch any juice.

When the couscous is cooked, stir in the nuts and herbs and a little salt and pepper.

Mix together the pomegranate seeds and juice and lemon zest and juice. Spoon over the couscous just before serving.

For broiled marinated haloumi, to serve as an accompaniment, slice 8 oz haloumi into 8 pieces and marinate in the juice of 1 lemon, a dash of olive oil, and 1 fresh green chili, finely chopped. Leave for 20 minutes before broiling until brown and crisp. Serve 2 slices per person on top of the pilaf.

lima bean & potato casserole

Serves **4**
Preparation time **15 minutes**
Cooking time **1 hour**

olive oil spray
1 mild **Spanish onion**, sliced
2 **garlic cloves**, crushed
7 oz **potatoes**, peeled and
   diced
1 small **turnip**, peeled and
   thinly sliced
2 x 13½ oz cans **lima beans**,
   rinsed and drained
6 tablespoons **red wine**
13 oz can **chopped tomatoes**
1 cup **vegetable stock**
pinch of **paprika**
1 **bay leaf**
2 tablespoons chopped **flat
   leaf parsley**
salt and pepper

Spray a flameproof casserole pan with oil, add the onion, and cook over low heat for 10 minutes. Add the garlic, potatoes, turnip, and lima beans and stir to combine.

Add all the remaining ingredients, season to taste, and bring to a simmer.

Transfer the casserole to in a preheated oven, 350°F, and cook for 45 minutes. Check the seasoning, remove the bay leaf, and sprinkle with chopped parsley. Serve with a green salad, if desired.

For lima bean & tomato casserole, omit the potatoes and turnips and instead use 2 sliced onions, 3 x 13½ oz cans lima beans and 2 x 13 oz cans chopped tomatoes. Add several sprigs of fresh oregano and simmer on the burner for 15 minutes, rather than in the oven. Serve warm with crusty bread.

vietnamese rolls with peanut dip

Serves **4**

Preparation time **20 minutes**,
   plus soaking

Cooking time **5 minutes**

2 oz **rice vermicelli noodles**

12 **rice paper rounds**

½ **cucumber**, seeded and
   shredded

1 **carrot**, shredded

2 **scallions**, shredded

¼ cup **mint leaves**, left whole

¾ cup **bean sprouts**

2 **Chinese cabbage leaves**,
   shredded

⅓ cup **cashew nuts**, chopped
   and roasted

Dipping sauce

2 tablespoons **hoisin sauce**

2 tablespoons **chili sauce**

2 tablespoons natural
   peanuts, chopped
   and roasted

1 **red chili**, finely chopped

Cook the noodles according to the instructions on the package. Drain and set aside.

Soak the rice paper rounds in cold water for 3 minutes or until softened. Do not soak for too long or they will fall apart.

Mix together the cucumber, carrot, scallions, mint, bean sprouts, Chinese cabbage, and cashew nuts.

Make the sauce by mixing the hoisin and chili sauces with the peanuts and chili.

Put a generous spoonful of vegetables in the center of each rice paper round, roll it up tightly and fold over the ends. Serve the rolls immediately with the dipping sauce.

For chili & honey dipping sauce, replace the hoisin sauce with 2 tablespoons soy sauce and the chili sauce with 2 tablespoons honey. Omit the peanuts and combine with 1 finely chopped red chili.

sweet potato & cheese frittata

Serves **4**

Preparation time **10 minutes**

Cooking time **20 minutes**

1 lb **sweet potatoes**, sliced

1 teaspoon **olive oil**

5 **scallions**, sliced

2 tablespoons chopped **cilantro**

4 large **eggs**, beaten

4 oz round **goat cheese with rind**, cut into 4 slices

pepper

Put the sweet potato slices in a saucepan of boiling water and cook for 7–8 minutes or until just tender, then drain.

Heat the oil in a medium nonstick skillet, add the scallions and sweet potato slices and fry for 2 minutes.

Stir the cilantro into the beaten eggs, season with plenty of pepper and pour into the pan. Arrange the slices of goat cheese on top and continue to cook for 3–4 minutes until almost set.

Put the pan under a preheated hot broiler and cook for 2–3 minutes until golden and bubbling. Serve immediately, with a green salad if desired.

For butternut squash & feta frittata, replace the sweet potatoes with 1 lb cubed butternut squash. Sprinkle feta cheese on top of the frittata in place of the goat cheese.

roasted vegetable & potato bake

Serves **4**

Preparation time **15 minutes**

Cooking time **45 minutes**

1 tablespoon **olive oil**

7 oz **waxy potatoes**, cut into
chunks

1 **yellow bell pepper**, cored,
seeded, and roughly diced

2 **red bell peppers**, cored,
seeded, and roughly diced

4 **garlic cloves**, halved

2 tablespoons chopped
thyme

2 **bay leaves**

4 oz **feta cheese**

2 tablespoons chopped **mint**

2 tablespoons chopped **dill**

3 tablespoons **extra light
cream cheese**

1 **beefsteak tomato**, roughly
diced

3 small **zucchini**, halved
lengthwise

salt and pepper

Toss the oil with the potatoes, peppers, garlic, thyme,
and bay leaves in an ovenproof serving dish and cook
in a preheated oven, 400°F, for 30 minutes.

Mash together the feta, mint, dill, and cream cheese
and season to taste.

Add the tomato and zucchini to the vegetables. Spoon
the feta and cream cheese mixture over the vegetables
and bake for an additional 15 minutes until golden.
Garnish with thyme sprigs and serve immediately, with
a green salad.

For vegetable crumble, use 1½ cups rye bread
crumbs, 2 tablespoons chopped fennel, and 2 oz
finely grated Wensleydale cheese and mash together.
Spoon over the vegetables and bake as above.

oven-baked ratatouille

Serves **4**
Preparation time **25 minutes**
Cooking time **about 1¼ hours**

1 tablespoon **olive oil**
1 **onion**, chopped
2 **garlic cloves**, finely
   chopped
1 **fennel bulb**, about 8 oz,
   diced
3 different colored **bell
   peppers**, cored, seeded,
   and diced
2 **zucchini**, about 10 oz in
   total, diced
13 oz can **chopped tomatoes**
⅔ cup **vegetable stock**
1 teaspoon **superfine sugar**
salt and pepper

Goat cheese topping
1 **baguette,** about 5 oz,
   thinly sliced
4 oz **goat cheese with chives**

Heat the oil over a high heat in a large, nonstick skillet, add the onion and fry, stirring, for 5 minutes or until lightly browned. Add the garlic and remaining fresh vegetables and fry for an additional 2 minutes.

Stir in the tomatoes, stock, sugar, and a little seasoning. Bring to a boil, stirring, then transfer to a deep ovenproof dish. Cover the top of the dish with foil and bake in a preheated oven, 375°F, for 45–60 minutes until the vegetables are tender.

When the vegetables are almost ready, broil one side of the bread slices. Slice the cheese and add one slice to each untoasted side of bread. Remove the foil from the ratatouille, stir the vegetables, and top with the toasts, cheese side up.

Put the ratatouille under a preheated hot broiler for 4–5 minutes until the cheese is just beginning to melt. Spoon into shallow bowls and serve with an arugula salad, if desired.

For herb cobbler, to serve as an accompaniment, make biscuit dough by sifting together 2 cups flour with ½ teaspoon baking powder and combine with ¼ cup butter and 2 finely chopped scallions. Add a pinch of dried herbs and bake in a round topped with a little grated mature cheddar cheese for 20 minutes, while the ratatouille is baking. Cut into wedges and serve with the ratatouille.

asparagus & dolcelatte risotto

Serves **4**
Preparation time **10 minutes**
Cooking time **about 25 minutes**

1 teaspoon **olive oil**
1 small **onion**, finely chopped
10 oz **asparagus**, halved and the stem end finely sliced
1¾ cups **risotto rice**
2 tablespoons **dry white wine**
5 cups **vegetable stock**
3 oz **dolcelatte cheese**, chopped
2 tablespoons chopped **parsley**

Heat the oil in a large, nonstick skillet, add the onion and sliced asparagus, reserving the tips, and fry for 2–3 minutes until beginning to soften.

Add the rice and coat in the oil, then add the wine and allow it to be absorbed.

Bring the stock to a boil and add it to the rice mixture, ladle by ladle, allowing the liquid to be absorbed before adding any more. With the last addition of stock (which should be about 20 minutes from when you started), add the asparagus tips.

Once all the stock has been absorbed, gently stir through the remaining ingredients and, if desired, serve the risotto with an arugula and tomato salad.

For arugula risotto, quickly fry the onion and cook 1½ cups risotto rice in 5 cups stock as above, then stir in 1¼ cups torn arugula leaves when the rice is cooked. Use whole leaves to garnish.

salads

thai noodle salad

Serves **4**

Preparation time **15 minutes**, plus cooling

Cooking time **5 minutes**

7 oz **flat rice noodles**

1 tablespoon **sesame oil**

4 oz **pork tenderloin**, diced

1 tablespoon **light soy sauce**

1 tablespoon **sesame seeds**, toasted

2 **shallots**, peeled and chopped

12 **baby corn ears**, chopped

1 cup **bean sprouts**

⅓ cup **peanuts**, chopped and toasted

4 tablespoons chopped **cilantro**

Lime and coconut dressing

2 **garlic cloves**, crushed

2 tablespoons **lime juice**

½ **lemon grass** stalk, finely chopped

½ **red chili**, chopped

½ cup **reduced-fat coconut milk**

1 tablespoon **Thai fish sauce**

salt

Cook the noodles according to the instructions on the package. Drain.

Meanwhile, heat the sesame oil in a skillet and gently fry the diced pork for 1–2 minutes. Stir in the soy sauce and cook for 1–2 minutes or until the pork is sticky and coated. Set aside to cool.

Stir the sesame seeds, shallots, corn, and bean sprouts into the cold pork.

Make the dressing by mixing together all the ingredients in a bowl.

Stir the dressing through the noodles and pork, add the peanuts and cilantro and serve immediately.

For rice & shrimp salad, cook 1¼ cups rice according to the package instructions. Replace the pork with 12 oz peeled, cooked shrimp. Rather than frying the shrimp, simply stir them through the soy sauce.

puy lentil & goat cheese salad

Serves **4**

Preparation time **10 minutes**

Cooking time **about 30 minutes**

2 teaspoons **olive oil**

2 teaspoons **cumin seeds**

2 **garlic cloves**, crushed

2 teaspoons grated **fresh ginger root**

½ cup **Puy lentils**

3 cups **vegetable stock**

2 tablespoons chopped **mint**

2 tablespoons chopped **cilantro**

½ **lime**

3 cups **baby spinach** leaves

4 oz **goat cheese**

pepper

Heat the oil in a saucepan over medium heat, add the cumin seeds, garlic, and ginger and cook for 1 minute. Add the lentils and cook for an additional minute.

Add the stock to the pan, stir, and simmer for 25 minutes, until all the liquid is absorbed and the lentils are tender. Check the seasoning. Remove the pan from the heat and set aside to cool. Stir in the mint and cilantro and add a squeeze of lime.

Arrange the spinach leaves in individual bowls, top with a quarter of the lentils and the goat cheese, and serve sprinkled with black pepper.

For lentil & egg salad, replace the cheese with 4 hard-cooked eggs, quartered. Make the salad as above and sprinkle with ⅓ cup green olives, chopped, and the eggs.

trout & cracked wheat salad

Serves **4**

Preparation time **10 minutes**,
   plus cooling

Cooking time **20 minutes**

2 cups **cracked wheat**

1 tablespoon **olive oil**

12 oz **smoked trout fillet**,
   flaked

1 **cucumber**, seeded and
   diced

3 cups **baby spinach leaves**,
   washed

1 **red onion**, sliced

7 oz can **green lentils**, rinsed
   and drained

3 oz **sugar snap peas**, finely
   sliced

**Lemon and poppy seed
   dressing**

grated zest of 2 **lemons**

4 tablespoons **lemon juice**

2 tablespoons **poppy seeds**

2 tablespoons chopped **dill**

salt and pepper

Cook the cracked wheat according to the instructions on the package. Stir through the oil and set aside.

Stir the trout into the cooled cracked wheat, then add the cucumber, spinach, red onion, lentils, and peas.

Make the dressing by mixing together the lemon zest and juice, poppy seeds, and dill. Season the dressing to taste and just before serving drizzle it over the salad.

For smoked mackerel salad, use 12 oz smoked mackerel instead of the smoked trout. Serve with a horseradish dressing instead of the lemon and poppy seed, combining 2 tablespoons creamed horseradish with 4 tablespoons mild yogurt.

chicken, pineapple, & rice salad

Serves **4**

Preparation time **40 minutes**

4 boneless, skinless **chicken breasts**, about 4 oz each, cooked

1 cup **wholegrain rice**, cooked

½ **pineapple**, chopped

1 **red bell pepper**, chopped

3 **scallions**, chopped

⅓ cup **dried blueberries**

salt and pepper

Mustard dressing

3 tablespoons **sunflower oil**

4 tablespoons **Dijon mustard**

1 tablespoon **red wine vinegar**

Dice the chicken and put it in a large bowl with the rice. Stir in the pineapple, bell pepper, scallions, and blueberries. Season to taste with salt and pepper.

Make the dressing by mixing all the ingredients with 2 tablespoons water. Season to taste.

Spoon the dressing over the chicken mixture and serve straightaway.

For walnut, flageolet bean, & blueberry rice salad,

replace the pineapple and dried blueberries with 1⅓ cups fresh blueberries and add ⅔ cup fresh walnut halves and a 13½ oz can flageolet beans, drained and rinsed. Mix together and season as above.

bean, kabanos, & pepper salad

Serves **4**

Preparation time **10 minutes**, plus cooling

Cooking time **20 minutes**

3 **red bell peppers**, cored and seeded

1 **red chili**, seeded and sliced

1 tablespoon **olive oil**

1 **onion**, sliced

3 oz **kabanos sausage**, thinly sliced

2 x 13½ oz cans **lima** or **flageolet beans**, rinsed and drained

1 tablespoon **balsamic vinegar**

2 tablespoons chopped **cilantro**

Put the peppers on a baking sheet, skin side up, and cook under a preheated hot broiler for 8–10 minutes until the skins are blackened. Cover with damp paper towels. When the peppers are cool enough to handle, remove the skins and slice the flesh.

Heat the oil in a nonstick skillet, add the onion and fry for 5–6 minutes until soft. Add the kabanos sausage and fry for 1–2 minutes until crisp.

Mix together the beans and balsamic vinegar, then add the onion and kabanos mixture and the peppers and chili. Serve the salad with walnut bread, if desired.

For bean, pepper, & olive salad with haloumi, omit the kabanos sausage and mix ⅓ cup halved pitted black olives with the beans. Slice and broil 3 oz haloumi. Divide the salad among bowls and top with the haloumi.

Italian broiled chicken salad

Serves **4**

Preparation time **20 minutes**, plus cooling

Cooking time **about 15 minutes**

4 **chicken breasts**, about 4 oz each

8 small **plum tomatoes**, halved

olive oil spray

13 oz **new potatoes**

2 cups **baby spinach leaves**

salt and pepper

Italian dressing

10 **basil leaves**, chopped

2 tablespoons chopped **oregano**

1 **garlic clove**, chopped

1 tablespoon **olive oil**

2 tablespoons **lemon juice**

1 tablespoon **Dijon mustard**

grated zest of 1 **lemon**

Use a sharp knife to cut each chicken breast in half horizontally. Arrange the 8 pieces of chicken on a foil-lined broiler pan with the tomatoes. Season and spray with oil.

Cook the chicken under a preheated hot broiler for about 2 minutes or until it is just cooked and still succulent. Set aside to cool, then cut the chicken into bite-size pieces.

Meanwhile, steam or boil the potatoes. Set aside to cool, then slice into rounds.

Make the dressing by mixing together all the ingredients.

Combine the chicken, spinach, tomatoes, and potatoes in a serving dish. Just before serving, pour over the dressing.

For Italian vegetable salad, omit the chicken and boil 7 oz trimmed fine green beans for 3 minutes. Toast 2 tablespoons pine nuts briefly in the oven. Prepare the salad as above, combining the beans with the other ingredients. Toss with the Italian dressing and serve topped with the pine nuts and shavings of Parmesan cheese.

red roasted pork & quinoa salad

Serves **4**

Preparation time **10 minutes,**
  plus cooling

Cooking time **15 minutes**

1 tablespoon **sunflower oil**

2 **star anise**

1 tablespoon **Demerara
  sugar**

1 tablespoon **five spice
  powder**

1 tablespoon **soy sauce**

1 tablespoon **paprika**

1 lb **pork tenderloin**, thinly
  sliced

1½ cups **quinoa**

7 oz **sugar snap peas**, halved

4 **scallions**, chopped

1 head of **Chinese cabbage**,
  shredded

dill sprigs (optional)

Yogurt dressing

½ cup **Greek** or **whole milk
  yogurt**

2 tablespoons **water**

2 tablespoons chopped **dill**

salt and pepper

Mix together the oil, star anise, sugar, five spice powder, soy sauce, and paprika. Add the pork and stir to coat, then transfer to a roasting pan. Cover and cook in a preheated oven, 350°F, for 15 minutes or until just cooked but not dry. Remove, uncover, and set aside to cool.

Meanwhile, cook the quinoa according to the instructions on the package. Set aside to cool.

Toss the quinoa with the peas, scallion, and Chinese cabbage. Add the pork and the cooking juices, if desired.

Make the dressing by mixing together all the ingredients. Season to taste, drizzle the dressing over the salad and serve sprinkled with dill sprigs, if desired.

For tandoori spiced pork, mix 2 tablespoons tandoori spice with 6 tablespoons yogurt, pour over the pork tenderloin, and roast as above. For a raita style dressing to accompany the pork, use ½ white sliced cabbage mixed with 1¼ cups yogurt and 1 grated carrot. Add 1 tablespoon roasted cumin seeds to the dressing and mix well.

italian broccoli & egg salad

Serves **4**
Preparation time **10 minutes**
Cooking time **8 minutes**

10 oz **broccoli**

2 small **leeks**, about 10 oz
  in total, trimmed, slit and
  well rinsed

4 tablespoons **lemon juice**

2 tablespoons **olive oil**

2 teaspoons **honey**

1 tablespoon **capers**, well
  drained

2 tablespoons chopped
  tarragon

4 hard-cooked **eggs**

salt and pepper

Cut the broccoli into florets and thickly slice the stems
and the leeks. Put the broccoli in the top of a steamer,
cook for 3 minutes, add the leeks and cook for another
2 minutes.

Mix together the lemon juice, oil, honey, capers, and
tarragon in a salad bowl and season to taste.

Shell and roughly chop the eggs.

Add the broccoli and leeks to the dressing, toss
together and sprinkle with the chopped eggs. Garnish
with tarragon sprigs, if desired, and serve warm with
extra thickly sliced whole-wheat bread.

For broccoli, cauliflower, & egg salad, use 5 oz
broccoli and 5 oz cauliflower instead of 10 oz
broccoli. Cut the cauliflower into small florets and
steam with the broccoli. Serve with a blue cheese
dressing made by mixing together 3 oz blue cheese,
6 chopped sun-dried tomatoes, and 3 tablespoons
balsamic vinegar.

turkey skewers & bulghur salad

Serves **4**
Preparation time **10 minutes**,
  plus marinating
Cooking time **20 minutes**

2 tablespoons **sunflower oil**
2 tablespoons **lemon juice**
1 teaspoon **paprika**
3 tablespoons chopped **flat
  leaf parsley**, plus extra to
  garnish
13 oz **turkey breast**, diced
salt and pepper

Bulghur salad
1¾ cups **chicken stock**
1¼ cups **bulghur wheat**
13½ oz can **green lentils**,
  rinsed and drained
½ **cucumber**
10 **cherry tomatoes**
½ cup **mint**, chopped
lemon wedges, to garnish

Hummus dressing
4 tablespoons **hummus**
1 tablespoon **lemon juice**

Presoak 8 wooden skewers in warm water. Mix together the oil, lemon juice, paprika, and parsley, and season to taste. Add the turkey and turn to coat thoroughly. Set aside for at least 20 minutes.

Drain the turkey (discard any marinade) and thread the pieces onto the skewers. Cook under a preheated hot broiler, turning once or twice, for 10 minutes or until cooked through.

Meanwhile, bring the stock to a boil and cook the bulghur wheat according to the package instructions. Drain and spread out to cool. Stir in the green lentils, cucumber, tomatoes, and mint.

Make the dressing by combining the hummus with the lemon juice and 1 tablespoon water.

Serve the turkey skewers with the bulghur wheat salad, garnished with lemon wedges and flat leaf parsley. Offer the dressing separately.

For pasta shapes salad, instead of the bulghur salad, replace the lentils and bulghur wheat with 8 oz cooked small pasta shapes. Instead of the hummus dressing, mix together ¾ cup low-fat yogurt with 1½ cups each chopped fresh basil and mint.

spiced orange & avocado salad

Serves **4**

Preparation time **10 minutes**

4 large juicy **oranges**

2 small ripe **avocados**, peeled
  and pitted

2 teaspoons **cardamom pods**

3 tablespoons **light olive oil**

1 tablespoon **honey**

generous pinch of **ground
  allspice**

2 teaspoons **lemon juice**

salt and pepper

watercress sprigs, to garnish

Cut the skin and the white membrane off the oranges. Working over a bowl to catch the juice, cut between the membranes to remove the segments.

Slice the avocados and toss gently with the orange segments. Pile onto serving plates.

Reserve a few whole cardamom pods for decoration. Crush the remaining pods to extract the seeds and pick out and discard the pods. Mix the seeds with the oil, honey, allspice, lemon juice, salt and pepper, and reserved orange juice.

Garnish with watercress, spoon the dressing over the top, and serve.

For grapefruit & avocado salad, replace the oranges with 2 large grapefruits and add 1 cup blueberries. Replace the ground allspice with 1 teaspoon nutmeg.

chili beef salad with cilantro

Serves **4**
Preparation time **20 minutes**
Cooking time **10 minutes**

13 oz **beef sirloin steaks**
4 **wheat tortillas**, cut into
  8 wedges
2 cups **baby spinach leaves**,
  washed
salt and pepper

Lime and cilantro dressing
⅓ cup **cilantro leaves**
2 tablespoons **lime juice**
1 tablespoon **sunflower oil**
1 **garlic clove**, crushed
1 **red chili**, finely chopped

Season the beef. Heat a large skillet and sear the beef over high heat until it is cooked but still pink. This will take about 2 minutes each side, depending on thickness. Set aside at room temperature.

Grill the tortillas under a preheated hot broiler for about 5 minutes, shaking the pan frequently, until they are crispy. Set aside to cool.

Meanwhile, make the dressing by combining all the ingredients.

Thinly slice the beef and arrange it on the spinach leaves. Spoon over the dressing just before serving with the tortilla wedges.

For crushed new potatoes with cilantro dressing, to serve as an accompaniment, boil 1½ lb new potatoes for 12 minutes until soft. Crush, not mash, the potatoes and serve drizzled with the cilantro dressing and a handful of pine nuts.

herby lima bean salad

Serves **4**
Preparation time **10 minutes**

1½ lb jar *judion de la granja
   beans* or **lima beans**, rinsed
   and drained
1 oz **Serrano ham**, chopped
4 ripe **tomatoes**, sliced
1 mild **Spanish onion**, sliced

Herb dressing
1 cup chopped **flat leaf
   parsley**
1 cup chopped **mint**
grated zest and juice of
   2 lemons
2 **garlic cloves**, crushed
1 tablespoon **olive oil**
2 teaspoons **cider vinegar**
1 teaspoon chopped
   anchovies (optional)
salt and pepper

Arrange the beans and ham in a serving dish with the sliced tomatoes and onion.

Make the dressing by mixing together the parsley, mint, lemon zest and juice, garlic, oil, and vinegar. Season to taste and stir in the anchovies, if using.

Drizzle the dressing over the beans and ham and serve.

For herby chickpea & tuna salad, use 2 x 13½ oz cans chickpeas and a 6½ oz can tuna instead of the lima beans and ham. Drain the chickpeas and tuna and toss together, then add the tomatoes and onion and divide among serving dishes. Mix the dressing and pour over the salad. Serve with slices of ciabatta.

salmon & quails' egg salad

Serves **4**
Preparation time **15 minutes**
Cooking time **3–6 minutes**

12 **quails' eggs**
7 oz baby **asparagus**, ends
   trimmed
1 red **oak-leaf lettuce**
1 head **curly endive**
8 oz **smoked salmon**
juice of **1 lime**
salt and pepper
a few **chervil** sprigs, to
   garnish

Lemon dressing
grated zest and juice of
   2 **unwaxed lemons**
½ teaspoon **English mustard**
1 **egg yolk**
6 tablespoons **olive oil**

Boil the eggs for 3 minutes, then drain and cool them under cold running water. Peel the eggs and place in salted water and set aside until required.

Meanwhile, put the asparagus in a pan of boiling water and cook over a medium heat for 3–5 minutes or until tender. Drain, refresh under cold running water, and set aside.

Make the dressing by putting the lemon zest and juice, mustard, and egg yolk in a food processor or blender. Process briefly to combine the ingredients thoroughly, then, on a low speed, add the oil in a steady stream. Season to taste.

Separate the lettuce and endive leaves, removing any tough stalks, and wash thoroughly. Put the leaves in a bowl and add two-thirds of the dressing. Toss to distribute the dressing evenly, then arrange in the center of 4 serving plates.

Divide the salmon into 4 and arrange it on the salad leaves. Sprinkle with lime juice. Halve the eggs and arrange them over the salad. Drizzle with the remaining dressing, garnish with chervil sprigs and serve.

For trout & egg salad, use 4 hens' eggs instead of the quails' eggs, boiling them for about 10 minutes. Replace the smoked salmon with the same quantity of smoked trout fillets. Skin the trout and flake the flesh, discarding any bones. Sprinkle the trout over the leaves, then quarter the eggs and arrange on top.

squid salad with greek potatoes

Serves **4**

Preparation time **30 minutes**

Cooking time **2 minutes**

1 lb prepared **squid**

2 tablespoons **lemon juice**

2 tablespoons **olive oil**

1 **garlic clove**, chopped

2 tablespoons chopped **flat leaf parsley**

1 lb **new potatoes**, cooked

12 **cherry tomatoes**, halved

4 **scallions**, chopped

salt and pepper

lemon wedges, to serve

Cut the squid bodies in half widthwise, then in half again so that they open out into squares. Score on one side and mix with the lemon juice and some seasoning.

Cook the squid in a preheated heavy skillet or griddle pan over high heat for 1 minute on each side. Stir in the oil, garlic, and parsley, then remove from the heat and set aside to cool.

Spoon the squid and dressing over the potatoes, tomatoes, and scallions and serve with some lemon wedges.

For shrimp salad with green olives, use 1 lb peeled raw jumbo shrimp instead of the squid. Defrost if frozen and rinse under cold water. Season and mix with the lemon juice. Cook on a griddle pan as for the squid, then finish as above, adding ⅓ cup pitted green olives, sliced, to the cooked shrimp. Sprinkle with grated lemon zest before serving.

crab & grapefruit salad

Serves **4**

Preparation time **10 minutes**

13 oz **white crabmeat**

1 **pink grapefruit**, peeled and
  sliced

1¼ cups **arugula**

3 **scallions**, sliced

7 oz **snow peas**, halved

salt and pepper

Watercress dressing

2 cups **watercress**, tough
  stalks removed

1 tablespoon **Dijon mustard**

2 tablespoons **olive oil**

To serve

4 **chapattis**

lime wedges

Combine the crabmeat, grapefruit, arugula, scallions,
and snow peas in a serving dish. Season to taste.

Make the dressing by blending together the
watercress, mustard, and oil. Season with salt.

Toast the chapattis. Stir the dressing into the salad
and serve with the toasted chapattis and lime wedges
on the side.

For shrimp, potato, & asparagus salad, substitute
13 oz cooked peeled shrimp for the crab and 4 oz
cooked asparagus for the grapefruit, and add 7 oz
cooked and cooled potatoes.

spring vegetable salad

Serves **4**
Preparation time **10 minutes**
Cooking time **10 minutes**

1⅛ cups fresh or frozen **peas**
7 oz **asparagus**, trimmed
7 oz **sugar snap peas**
2 **zucchini**, cut into long, thin
   ribbons
1 **fennel bulb**, thinly sliced
grated zest and juice of
   1 **lemon**
1 teaspoon **Dijon mustard**
1 teaspoon **honey**
1 tablespoon chopped **flat
   leaf parsley**
2 tablespoons **olive oil**

Garlic bread
4 **ciabatta rolls**, halved
1 **garlic clove**

Put the peas, asparagus, and sugar snap peas in a saucepan of salted boiling water and simmer for 3 minutes. Drain, then refresh under cold running water.

Transfer the vegetables to a large bowl with the zucchini ribbons and fennel and mix together.

Beat together the lemon zest and juice, mustard, honey, parsley, and half the oil in a separate bowl. Toss this dressing through the vegetables.

Rub the cut sides of the rolls with the garlic clove, drizzle over the remaining oil, then place the rolls on a baking sheet under a preheated hot broiler and toast on both sides. Serve with the salad.

For poached eggs on spicy toasts, remove the crusts from 4 slices multigrain bread. Use 1 tablespoon chili-infused oil to brush each side of the bread and broil as above. Poach 4 eggs in a pan of simmering water with 1 teaspoon vinegar added. Drain, trim, and serve on the toasts, with the salad.

shrimp, pea shoot, & quinoa salad

Serves **4**
Preparation time **10 minutes**
Cooking time **10 minutes**

1½ cups **quinoa**
3 oz **snow peas**, blanched
    and halved
7 oz **asparagus spears**,
    cooked, cooled, and cut into
    bite-size pieces
2 oz **pea shoots**
13 oz cooked **jumbo shrimp**,
    shells removed
salt and pepper

Fruit and nut dressing
2 tablespoons **olive oil**
2 tablespoons **lemon juice**
3 tablespoons **dried**
    cranberries
½ cup **hazelnuts**, chopped
    and toasted

Cook the quinoa according to the instructions on the package. Set aside to cool.

Stir the snow peas and asparagus through the quinoa.

Make the dressing by mixing together the oil, lemon juice, cranberries, and hazelnuts.

Spoon the pea shoots and shrimp over the quinoa, drizzle with the dressing, and serve.

For shrimp, bulghur wheat, & nut salad, use 1½ cups bulghur wheat instead of the quinoa. For a nuttier dressing, toast ¼ cup slivered almonds in a dry pan with the hazelnuts, then mix with the olive oil and the zest and juice of 1 orange.

smoked chicken & onion salad

Serves **4**

Preparation time **10 minutes**

10 oz skinless **smoked chicken breast**

2 **red onions**, finely sliced

10 **cherry tomatoes**, halved

¼ cup **pumpkin seeds**, roasted

2 cups **mixed salad** leaves

salt and pepper

Avocado dressing

1 **avocado**, peeled and diced

2 tablespoons **lime juice**

1 tablespoon **Dijon mustard**

Dice or shred the smoked chicken. Rinse the red onions in water.

Make the dressing by blending together the avocado, lime juice, mustard, and seasoning.

Toss together the chicken, onion, tomatoes, pumpkin seeds, and salad leaves, drizzle over the dressing and serve.

For smoked chicken, broccoli, & pasta salad,

cook 8 oz rigatoni in boiling salted water for about 12 minutes, until tender. Add 8 oz broccoli broken into tiny florets for the final 3 minutes cooking. The broccoli should be very lightly cooked. Drain well and rinse under cold water. Drain again. Prepare the salad as above, without tossing in the leaves. Toss the pasta and broccoli with the chicken mixture. Arrange the leaves in bowls and top with the pasta salad.

desserts

mango & passion fruit trifle

Serves **4**

Preparation time **10 minutes**, plus chilling

4 **ladyfingers**

⅔ cup **nonfat yogurt**

¾ cup **half-fat sour cream**

4 **passion fruit**

1 **mango**, peeled, pitted, and diced

Break each ladyfinger into 4 pieces and arrange them in 4 tumblers.

Mix together the yogurt and sour cream. Remove the seedy pulp from the passion fruit and set aside.

Spoon a little passion fruit pulp over the ladyfingers and then add about half of the mango pieces.

Pour about half the sour cream mix over the fruit and top with the remaining mango.

Top with the remaining sour cream mix and arrange the rest of the passion fruit on top. Refrigerate for up to 1 hour or serve immediately.

For pineapple & strawberry trifle, replace the mango with 1¼ cups peeled, diced pineapple and replace the passion fruit with 1 cup halved strawberries. You can also use any of the wide range of frozen fruit available, but make sure the fruit is fully thawed first. Continue as above.

st clement's cheesecake

Serves **10**
Preparation time **10 minutes**,
  plus cooling and chilling
Cooking time **50 minutes**

¼ cup **unsalted butter**
2 cups crushed **low-fat oat
  cookies**
2 cups **Quark**
½ cup **superfine sugar**
2 **eggs**
grated zest and juice of
  2 oranges
grated zest and juice of
  1 lemon
½ cup **golden raisins**
julidnnes of **orange and
  lemon peel**, to decorate

Lightly grease an 8 inch nonstick, removable-bottomed round cake pan.

Melt the butter in a saucepan, stir in the cookie crumbs, then press them over the base and side of the cake pan. Bake in a preheated oven, 300°F, for 10 minutes.

Beat together the remaining ingredients in a bowl, spoon the mixture into the cake pan and bake for 40 minutes until just firm. Turn off the oven and allow the cheesecake to cool in the oven for an hour.

Transfer the cheesecake to the refrigerator for 2 hours, then serve decorated with juliennes of orange and lemon peel. .

For lime & raspberry cheesecake, replace the oranges, lemon, and golden raisins with 2–3 drops vanilla extract and the grated zest and juice of 1 lime, then cook as above. Once chilled, decorate with 1 cup raspberries.

passion fruit panna cotta

Serves **4**

Preparation time **20 minutes**,
  plus setting

2 **gelatin leaves**
8 **passion fruit**
¾ cup **half-fat sour cream**
½ cup **nonfat yogurt**
1 teaspoon **superfine sugar**
vanilla bean, split

Soften the gelatin leaves in cold water. Halve the passion fruit and remove the seeds, working over a bowl to catch as much juice as you can. Reserve the seeds for decoration.

Combine the sour cream, yogurt, and passion fruit juice.

Put ¼ cup water in a small saucepan, add the sugar and the seeds from the vanilla bean and heat gently, stirring until the sugar has dissolved. Drain the gelatin and add to the pan. Stir until dissolved, then allow to cool to room temperature.

Mix the gelatin mixture into the sour cream, then pour into 4 ramekins or molds. Refrigerate for 6 hours or until set.

Turn the panna cotta out of their molds by briefly immersing each ramekin in very hot water. Spoon over the reserved seeds to decorate.

For coffee panna cotta, substitute 2 teaspoons strong coffee for the passion fruit and continue as for the recipe, using the vanilla bean. Decorate each panna cotta with chocolate coffee beans, if you desire.

raspberry shortbread mess

Serves **4**

Preparation time **5 minutes**

2½ cups **raspberries**, roughly
   chopped
4 **shortbread cookies**,
   roughly crushed
1¾ cups **low-fat yogurt**
2 tablespoons **confectioners'
   sugar** or **artificial
   sweetener**

Reserving a few raspberries for decoration, combine all the ingredients in a bowl. Spoon into 4 serving dishes.

Serve immediately, decorated with the reserved raspberries.

For Eton mess, use 4 meringue nests and 2 cups strawberries. Hull and halve or quarter the strawberries, then add them to the yogurt with the sugar or sweetener. Break the meringues into chunks and fold them through the yogurt, then pile into glasses and serve.

mango & passion fruit brûlée

Serves **4**

Preparation time **10 minutes**, plus chilling

Cooking time **2 minutes**

1 small **mango**, peeled, pitted, and thinly sliced

2 **passion fruit**, flesh scooped out

1¼ cups **low-fat plain yogurt**

¾ cup **low-fat sour cream**

1 tablespoon **confectioners' sugar**

few drops **vanilla extract**

2 tablespoons **Demerara sugar**

Arrange the mango slices in 4 ramekins.

Stir together the passion fruit flesh, yogurt, sour cream, confectioners' sugar, and vanilla extract in a bowl, then spoon the mixture over the mango. Tap each ramekin to level the surface.

Sprinkle over the Demerara sugar and cook the brûlées under a preheated hot broiler for 1–2 minutes until the sugar has melted. Chill for about 30 minutes, then serve.

For plum & peach brûlée, replace the mango with 2 sliced peaches. Continue as above, replacing the passion fruit with 4 firm but ripe chopped plums. Before broiling, top each ramekin with a piece of chopped crystallized ginger.

blueberry & lemon ice cream

Serves **4**

Preparation time **10 minutes**, plus freezing

3½ cups frozen **blueberries**

2 cups **nonfat yogurt**

1 cup **confectioners' sugar**, plus extra to decorate

grated zest of 2 **lemons**

1 tablespoon **lemon juice**

Reserve a few blueberries for decoration. Put the remainder of the blueberries in a food processor or blender with the yogurt, confectioners' sugar, and lemon zest and juice and process until smooth.

Spoon the mixture into a 2½ cup freezerproof container and freeze.

Eat when the frozen yogurt is softly frozen and easily spoonable. Before serving, decorate with the reserved blueberries and a sprinkling of confectioners' sugar. Use within 3 days.

For peach & black currant ice cream waffles, lightly toast 4 waffles, then top each with a sliced canned peach and drizzle with honey. Serve with black currant and lemon ice cream. Use 3½ cups frozen black currants in place of the blueberries. The same quantity of frozen blackberries or raspberries can also be used.

pears with maple syrup cookies

Serves **4**
Preparation time **20 minutes**
Cooking time **50 minutes**

2 **vanilla beans**, split
3 tablespoons **honey**
1½ cups **sweet white wine**
½ cup **superfine sugar**
4 hard **pears**, such as
  Packham or Comice, peeled,
  cored, and halved

Maple syrup cookies
2 tablespoons **reduced-fat
  sunflower spread**
2 tablespoons **maple syrup**
1 tablespoon **superfine sugar**
½ cup **all-purpose flour**
1 **egg white**

Combine the vanilla beans, honey, wine, sugar, and water in a saucepan large enough to hold all the pears. Heat until the sugar dissolves and then add the pears. Simmer for 30 minutes or until the pears are very tender. Remove the pears from the pan with a slotted spoon and set aside.

Simmer the syrup for about 15 minutes until it has reduced. Set aside with the pears until ready to serve.

Make the cookies. Beat together the sunflower spread, maple syrup, and sugar, then stir in the flour. Beat the egg white until softly peaking, then fold it into the mix.

Drop teaspoonfuls of the mixture onto a lightly greased cookie sheet, spacing the cookies well apart. Bake in a preheated oven, 400°F, for about 8 minutes until golden. Remove and transfer to a rack to cool.

Decorate the pears with a sliver of vanilla bean and serve with a little syrup drizzled over them and a cookie on the side.

For vanilla & rosewater peaches, replace the pears with the same quantity of peaches and poach in the syrup as above for about 20 minutes or until tender. Halved peaches will take less time. Remove the peaches and continue to simmer the syrup for about 15 minutes until it has reduced. Add 1–2 tablespoons rosewater, to taste, for a more fragrant syrup. Finish as above.

strawberries & meringue

Serves **4**
Preparation time **15 minutes**
Cooking time **2½ hours**

3 **egg whites**
⅔ cup **light brown sugar**
3 teaspoons **cornstarch**
1 teaspoon **white vinegar**
1 teaspoon **vanilla extract**
1⅔ cups **strawberries**, hulled
 and sliced

Line 4 tartlet pans or ramekins with nonstick parchment paper. Beat the egg whites until they form stiff peaks, then beat in the sugar, a spoonful at a time, making sure the sugar is incorporated between additions.

Fold in the cornstarch, vinegar, and vanilla extract.

Spoon the mixture into the pans or ramekins and cook in a preheated oven, 250°F, for 2½ hours.

Place the strawberries in an ovenproof dish and bake with the meringues for the last hour of the cooking time.

Spoon the strawberries and any cooking juices over the meringues to serve.

For baked nectarines with orange meringues, add the grated zest of 1 orange to the meringue with the cornstarch. Cut 2 peeled and pitted nectarines into thin slices and place in an ovenproof dish. Sprinkle with 2 tablespoons sugar and 1 tablespoon orange juice, then bake for 45 minutes with the meringues. Serve the fruit on the meringues.

lime & mango sorbet

Serves **4**

Preparation time **10 minutes**, plus freezing

Cooking time **5 minutes**

⅔ cup **superfine sugar**
1 cup **lime juice**
grated zest of 1 **lime**
3 **mangoes**, peeled and pitted
2 **egg whites**

Line a 2 lb loaf pan with plastic film or nonstick parchment paper. Put the sugar in a saucepan, add 1 cup water and warm gently until the sugar is dissolved. Remove from the heat and stir in the lime juice and grated zest.

Meanwhile, process the mango flesh to make a smooth puree, reserving four thin slices for the decoration. Stir the puree into the lime syrup and pour the mixture into the loaf pan. Freeze for at least 4 hours or overnight until solid.

Remove the sorbet from the pan and blend or process with the egg whites. Return the mixture to the pan and return to the freezer until firm. Eat within 3 days because the flavor of fresh fruit sorbets deteriorates quickly and this one has raw egg in it. Before serving, decorate each portion of sorbet with a thin slice of mango and serve with a couple of wafer cookies.

For passion fruit sorbet, omit the mangoes and use 1 cup passion fruit juice instead of the lime juice. The passion fruit juice can be bought or scooped from fresh fruit. To prepare fresh fruit, halve and scoop out the seeds and pulp into a sieve. Rub all the juice through the sieve, then discard the seeds.

mixed berry chocolate roulade

Serves **4**
Preparation time **20 minutes, plus cooling**
Cooking time **15 minutes**

3 large **eggs**
½ cup **superfine sugar**
½ teaspoon **chocolate extract**
½ cup **all-purpose flour**
¼ cup **cocoa**, plus extra to dust
⅔ cup **half-fat sour cream**
⅔ cup **nonfat yogurt**
¼ cup **confectioners' sugar**
1 tablespoon **chocolate sauce**
1½ cups **mixed berries**, chopped, plus extra to decorate

Grease and line a 12 x 8 inch jelly roll pan. Beat together the eggs and sugar until the mixer leaves a trail over the surface. Add the chocolate extract, sift in the flour and cocoa and fold in carefully.

Pour the mixture into the prepared pan. Bake in a preheated oven, 400°F, for 15 minutes.

Place a clean dish towel on the work surface and put a piece of nonstick parchment paper on top. When the sponge cake is cooked, turn it out onto the parchment paper, roll it up carefully, and allow to cool.

Mix together the sour cream, yogurt, confectioners' sugar, and chocolate sauce.

Unroll the roulade and spread the sour cream mix over it. Spoon the berries over the sour cream and roll up the roulade again. Dust with cocoa and serve immediately, decorated with extra berries.

For strawberry & vanilla roulade, omit the cocoa, increase the all-purpose flour to ¾ cup, and use ½ teaspoon vanilla extract instead of the chocolate extract. Use 1½ cups strawberries to fill the roulade and serve decorated with extra sliced strawberries, if desired.

frozen fruity yogurt

Serves **4**

Preparation time **15 minutes**, plus freezing

2½ cups fresh or frozen **raspberries**

3 **nectarines**, skinned, pitted, and chopped

2 tablespoons **confectioners' sugar**

1¾ cups **Greek** or **whole milk yogurt**

¾ cup **low-fat Greek** or **plain yogurt**

Put half the raspberries and nectarines in a food processor or blender and process until smooth.

Stir the puree and the rest of the fruit into the remaining ingredients, then transfer to a freezerproof container and freeze for 1 hour. Stir well, then return to the freezer and freeze until solid.

Serve the frozen yogurt in scoops, as you would ice cream. It will keep for up to 1 month in the freezer.

For frozen strawberry yogurt, gently cook 1⅔ cups hulled and chopped strawberries in 2 tablespoons red grape juice. Strain and stir the juice into 1 tablespoon crème de cassis, 2 tablespoons confectioners' sugar, and 1¼ cups plain yogurt. Continue as above.

very berry muffins

Makes **12**
Preparation time **15 minutes**
Cooking time **25 minutes**

2 cups **all-purpose flour**
4 tablespoons **superfine sugar**
1 tablespoon **baking powder**
1 **egg**, beaten
¾ cup **milk**
3 tablespoons **vegetable oil**
1½ cups **mixed berries**, roughly chopped

Mix together all of the ingredients, except the berries, to make a smooth dough. Fold in the berries.

Put nonstick paper bake cups in a 12-section muffin pan and spoon the mixture into the cups. Bake in a preheated oven, 350°F, for 25 minutes or until a toothpick comes out clean when inserted. Transfer to a cooling rack to cool.

For banana & pecan muffins, use 1½ cups chopped fresh banana instead of the berries, adding ¾ cup chopped pecan nuts with the bananas. Select firm but ripe bananas. Serve warm, drizzled with maple syrup.

chocolate & nectarine cake

Serves **6**
Preparation time **15 minutes**
Cooking time **45 minutes**

3 **nectarines**
3 oz **semisweet chocolate**,
   chopped
2 tablespoons **unsalted
   butter**
2 **egg yolks**
⅓ cup **superfine sugar**
½ teaspoon **chocolate extract**
4 **egg whites**
cocoa powder, for dusting

Line with parchment paper and grease a 10 inch cake pan. Put the nectarines in a bowl and pour over boiling water. Allow to stand for 1 minute, then peel off the skins. Halve the nectarines and remove the pits. Drain them well on paper towels and arrange, cut side down, in the prepared cake pan.

Put the chocolate and butter in a heatproof bowl and melt together over a pan of simmering water.

Beat together the egg yolks and sugar until the beater leaves a trail when lifted. The mix should be pale and quite stiff. Stir in the chocolate and chocolate extract.

Beat the egg whites until softly peaking. Stir a spoonful into the cake mix, then fold in the remainder. Spoon the mixture over the nectarines.

Bake the cake in a preheated oven, 350°F, for 45 minutes or until a toothpick inserted comes out clean. Serve warm or cold, dusted with cocoa powder.

For pear & chocolate soufflé cake, make a syrup by bringing ½ cup sugar to a boil in 1 cup water. Peel 3 pears and poach them in the syrup for 30 minutes at a gentle simmer. Drain the pears, reserving the syrup, then halve, core, and drain well. Use these instead of the nectarines in the cake as described above. Add the grated zest of 1 orange to the syrup and boil for 2 minutes, then serve with the cake.

cherry & cinnamon parfait

Serves **4**
Preparation time **10 minutes**,
   plus freezing
Cooking time **5 minutes**

11½ oz jar **morello cherries
   in syrup**
pinch of **ground cinnamon**
½ teaspoon **vanilla extract**
1 tablespoon **superfine sugar**
1 **egg yolk**
⅔ cup **half-fat sour cream**
4 **meringue nests**, broken
   into pieces
fresh cherries, to decorate

Drain the cherries and put 6 tablespoons of the syrup into a small saucepan. Stir the cinnamon, vanilla extract, and sugar into the syrup and heat for 5 minutes or until the sugar has dissolved. Set aside to cool.

Stir the egg yolk through the sour cream. Add the drained cherries to the syrup, then mix in the sour cream. Fold the meringue nests carefully through the mixture.

Transfer to a 1¼ cup freezerproof container and freeze for at least 4 hours. Eat within a day when the parfait will be softly frozen. Decorate with fresh cherries before serving.

For pineapple parfait, omit the morello cherries and instead drain and chop a 13 oz can sliced pineapple, adding to the syrup as above. Omit the egg yolk, and combine the pineapple, syrup, and sour cream. Fold through the meringue nests.

ricotta & maple syrup cheesecake

Serves **6**

Preparation time **20 minutes**, plus chilling

3 **gelatin** leaves

1½ cups crushed **reduced-fat graham crackers**

¼ cup **reduced-fat sunflower spread**, melted

1 cup **cottage cheese**

¾ cup **ricotta cheese**

2 **egg whites**

¼ cup **confectioners' sugar**, sifted

1½ tablespoons **lemon juice**

4 tablespoons **maple syrup**

To decorate

2 **oranges**, peeled and sliced

sprigs of **red currants**

Line an 8 inch springform pan with nonstick parchment paper. Soften the gelatin in cold water.

Mix together the cracker crumbs and melted sunflower spread and press into the prepared pan. Refrigerate.

Sieve together the cottage cheese and ricotta. Beat the egg whites until stiffly peaking, then beat in the confectioners' sugar until glossy.

Put the lemon juice and 3 tablespoons water in a saucepan over a low heat and stir in the gelatin until dissolved. Add to the ricotta mix with the maple syrup, then fold in the egg whites. Pour the mixture over the cracker base and refrigerate until set.

Decorate with the sliced oranges and sprigs of red currants before serving.

For raspberry & ricotta cheesecake with chocolate sauce, stir 2 cups raspberries into the pan with the ricotta mix, then make the cheesecake as above. To serve, melt 7 oz bittersweet chocolate with 4 tablespoons syrup and drizzle over the cheesecake.

banoffee mousse

Serves **4**

Preparation time **10 minutes**, plus setting

2 **gelatin** leaves

3 tablespoons **dulce de leche toffee sauce** or **fudge sauce**

½ cup **half-fat sour cream**

½ cup **honey-dipped banana chips**, chopped

4 **egg whites**

Soften the gelatin in cold water for 2 minutes.

Put the sauce in a small saucepan over gentle heat and stir in the gelatin until it has dissolved.

Stir the mixture into the sour cream and add the dried bananas, reserving a few for decoration.

Meanwhile, beat the egg whites until stiff, then fold through the toffee and banana mixture. Spoon into 4 glasses and decorate with the reserved banana chips and an extra dollop of sauce, if you desire.

For banana & hazelnut toffee creams, mash 2 fresh bananas and mix with the sauce and sour cream, omitting the gelatin and egg whites. Serve topped with ⅓ cup chopped toasted hazelnuts.

chocolate brownies

Makes **9**
Preparation time **10 minutes**
Cooking time **30 minutes**

½ cup **reduced-fat sunflower spread**
2 **eggs**
½ cup **light brown sugar**
¾ cup **self-rising flour**
½ cup **cocoa**, sifted, plus extra to decorate
2 oz **semisweet chocolate**, chopped
1 teaspoon **chocolate extract**
salt

Grease and line a 7 inch square deep cake pan.

Beat together the sunflower spread, eggs, and sugar. Stir in the flour and cocoa, then add the chocolate and chocolate extract. Stir in 1 teaspoon boiling water and a pinch of salt.

Transfer the mixture to the prepared pan and bake in a preheated oven, 375°F, for 30 minutes or until a toothpick comes out clean when inserted in the center. Allow to cool in the pan then cut into 9 squares. Dust with a little cocoa powder to serve.

For rum & raisin sauce, to go with the brownies, gently heat 1¼ cups milk in a saucepan with 2 tablespoons cornstarch, 4 tablespoons rum, and 4 tablespoons raisins. Add sugar to taste, before pouring the sauce over the cooled brownies.

summer fruit compôte

Serves **2**

Preparation time **5 minutes**, plus chilling

Cooking time **5 minutes**

2 cups **mixed summer fruit**, such as raspberries, blueberries, and strawberries, thawed if frozen

finely grated zest and juice of 1 large **orange**

1 tablespoon **red currant jelly**

1 cup **plain soy yogurt**, to serve

Put the fruit, orange zest and juice, and red currant jelly in a large saucepan. Cover and cook gently for 5 minutes or until the juices flow and the fruit is softened.

Remove the pan from the heat and set aside. When the fruit is cool, chill it and serve with soy yogurt.

For rhubarb, orange, & ginger compôte, omit the mixed summer fruit and red currant jelly and use 2 lb rhubarb cut in 1 inch pieces. Dissolve 1 cup superfine sugar in ⅔ cup water, bring to a boil and add the rhubarb. Simmer for about 5 minutes then allow to stand. Stir in the grated zest and juice of 1 orange with 3 tablespoons chopped preserved stem ginger, and chill.

index

234

acknowledgements

Executive editor: Nicky Hill
Editor: Fiona Robertson
Executive art editor: Penny Stock
Designer: Grade
Photographer: Lis Parsons
Food stylist: Alice Hart
Props stylist: Liz Hippisley
Senior production manager: Martin Croshaw

Special photography: © Octopus Publishing Group Limited/Lis Parsons
Other photography: © Octopus Publishing Group Limited/Frank Adam 129; /William Lingwood 31, 65, 69, 91, 123, 131, 135, 155, 175, 23; /Lis Parsons 49, 55, 59, 79, 127, 143, 151, 157, 163, 169, 191, 201, 207, 211, 221; /William Reavell 85, 95, 179; /Gareth Sambidge 17, 45, 101, 117, 125, 185